CONTENTS

MINE UMBRA / 1

A SINGLE PEARL / 63

COINCIDENCE BECOMES A ROOM / 89

MAGNETOSPHERE / 99
   PART 1 / 101
   PART 2 / 121

PUZZLE ME BACK / 141

WAVING AND HEAVING / 161

SEX AND MELANCHOLY / 177

   ABOUT THE AUTHOR / 185
   OTHER WORK BY TAD CORNELL / 187

BLUE HERON RISING

POEMS BY TAD CORNELL

Juggling Teacups Press
Kintnersville, PA

ISBN: 978-0-9908633-1-1 (paperback)
ISBN: 978-0-9908633-2-8 (Kindle)

Poems from MINE UMBRA have appeared in the following publications:
Poets' Attic, Polis, The River, Uses Literary Arts Magazine, and *Vortex: A Critical Revue*

Cover painting by George Inness "The Home of the Heron"

tadcornell6331@gmail.com
tadcornell.com

Juggling Teacups Press
www.jugglingteacupspress.com
Kintnersville, PA

MINE UMBRA

SELECTED POEMS 1985–1992

SANS DEPARTURE POINT

How is it that you know our north?
This place is as strange to us both.
Is it that you actually believe that tale,
the legend of magnetic trajectory,
told around the microwave and etched
where instead of bison we see printout?
It stands to reason, I suppose.
My head in the birth canal was pressed back,
my face blocking passage, so I'm told.
My knowledge of the way south has naught
to do with either Newton's or Adam's apple.
I've had no reference to sun, stars, or even moss
decor of trees to so consistently descend.
It is the forceps that bowed my head
to ram the gates of life, sans departure point,
left to flail for shadows and votive candles.

I STILL HAVE PHOTOS

I still have photos of a young priest
who instructed my mother and baptized me.
It was a spring day in Pennsylvania.
The smell of mud and wild berries.
Hats were still the fashion then.

There I am, Sydney Greenstreet,
bundled against chill in a knit cap.
The show ran another year in home movies
to close with Sydney trundled to Europe,
learning to walk on Queen Mary's deck.

When I became an altar boy, *uvum tutum meum,*
having learned that Noah drinks too much,
my dad went back to the States to bury his dad,
whose name I carry, and played the scene
of clutching made famous by Jacob and Esau.

I know your fillings and your dentures.
I am the head that surprises you in your plate.
My father's head is coughing in declensions.
We both are biting you. Our women
will have no peace outside the true church.

3

PASSIVE RESTRAINT

The technique is simple. You bring them to the ground
harmlessly. You hold on like a Nazi-hunter.
Your mind floats in a sensory deprivation tank
singing an Irish dirge and repeating Spanish
conjugations. You count on simple gravity to
anchor the soul's random fission. You propose
a kind of marriage; you plead for inner restraint.
The sky seems to open, and you see your last chance
riding the clouds, a child commanding names
and the motions of irresistible, blind elements.

EXPLORATORY SURGERY

He took himself into confidence like a Quaker.
He imagined himself a Pharaoh just before public
exhibition, x-rayed through the gauze.
He found himself intact. His members legible.
Someone knew better than to peel away the crust.
Winding himself into Goethe's salon, yet saving
his privates from surviving as paperweights,
the problem wound up protean. One atomic quark
had disguised itself as a quirk of fate
and history windowed itself for fast service,
dispensing hunter's stew to the amazed.

INHERITED FURNITURE

Inherited furniture is speaking volumes.
Two generations of diligent lounging
revealed in lumpy cushions and wood
all scratched unlocks a spiral code.

This chair is my dad all over.
It crouches like a bombardier above
his sights, alone with his hairline cross
against the target's topography grid.

This sofa is my mom, the prisoner of flight.
Its arms are frozen crests of waves
in opposite directions like a Red Sea passage
into forty years of dependence on manna.

And here, my grandmother's ashtray table.
She had a touch of Lady Macbeth.
She understood the ship of state.
Her drink was bourbon and her brand

Lucky Strikes. She liked recalling
the family's past dynastic captains.

One, an itinerant doctor, discovered copper
and ended financing Andrew Carnegie.

The roll-top desk is my grandfather.
He once defied his Latin teacher.
"Very good, Mr. Cornell."
"Good—hell, it's perfect," he said.

PSALM OF THE LAZY GATHERER

There I was, hammocked by the Butcher Bean Creek
on Mother's Day, slung between trunks whose leaves
mingle and adapt above in the struggle for light.

I was netted like the cast of miracles pulled ashore.
Lucky catch, these numbered organs that form a school
of purposeful fish programmed for spawning upstream.

I sustain that groaning the apostle once wrote of,
the one that all of nature shares in some universal
longing, and I so late on the stage of mercy's entrance.

I thought, I will sing for you one of Zion's songs,
those songs so large with choice, so fast along
the narrow margin, so sad remembering the catastrophe.

This one tells of the double bind when competing bliss
are neck and neck like parents you wish would divorce.
The horizon stretches in the badlands. Something bakes.

This figure standing on the precipice, tempter at his heels
and lame from angel wrestling, his vigilance itself strikes
the first chord on David's harp. He was not beneath nagging

like any shepherd; he would send his dog to harry strays.
The end of the earth was just beyond reach, setting crimson
in a larger masterpiece of permanent but indefinite design.

TO LISA

When I heard that you mourned my leaving
I thought I knew it was because you know
I really appreciate you. . .
and I think you honor me with your sorrow.
I think of all those times
I tried to talk you into going somewhere,
anywhere, just to see the blue sky again
or hear the swing band that proves
our daddies knew how to rock,
but especially the poetry group.
I guess you never could have sat still
for all the jibber jabber.
Did you know your smile is like the Mona Lisa?
Your smile alone would inspire us all,
but you never believed me about that.
Still, I wouldn't quit inviting you. . .
and that last time at the YMCA
was our best poetry group ever
because you came, thinking it was
an ordinary Universal Workout/ Olympic pool scene
like we usually do, real classy.

When you told me of the love you have for water
I had a sudden feeling you were growing,
like you had a poem in your hip pocket
and that's why you're always smiling.
And thinking of you swimming, growing, smiling. . .
that stuff lives in me. . . Let it live in you!
I give you permission to be happy without smiling,
or without swimming. . . But without growing?
Lisa, you have seen me frown on this.
So before you get too upset about my leaving,
keep in mind I have not really left.
My frown now lives in you, token of my love.

COUVADE OR NOT COUVADE

She told me of a birth dream,
how she plucked herself from drowning,
herself as fetus. . .
I had just had surgery on my left thigh.
It was nearly time for planting.

The adolescent lovers
running from the approaching storm,
their canopy streaming in their hands,
faces me now in the original by Cot.
Things Pre-Raphaelite seduce.

Displays of Mesopotamian artifacts
downstairs had struck me nostalgic.
These lovers see the humor in their storm.
Girls like these will visit some future
museum, see my pointy helmet, and laugh.

Their feet are bare, her dress is sheer,
his arm protects. She had just told him
her dream, how she plunged her hand
into water's black vacance without hope
and yet saved the helpless.

It was nearly time for planting.
The wound in his thigh was laced shut
with black thread. . .
He thought of a pun on the Greek words
for grapevine and scrotum.

Ideas hang like meat in a butcher shop,
forbidding, grotesque, random ideas.
They resist all numinous entry.
But I have my cyclotron to smash them
and my screen on which to read them.

I have my black thread to lead me out
and my barbs with which to hunt.
I have my seed and my furrowed ground.
She has her painting of our storm
and the endless, merciless exhibit space.

Couvade: n. cowardly inactivity/ a custom among some primitive peoples in
 accordance with which when a child is born, the father takes to bed as
 if bearing the child, cares for it, and submits himself to fasting,
 purification, or taboos.

THE FLOOR'S WARPING

Generalisimo of cottonballs,
of white out and Scotch tape,
pines in his knottiness.
Retail slaughter. No prisoners.
Apparitions from a tube he
squeezed beyond belief, now cowering.
Blast your command of shoe horns!
Wooden men belong to lost leather.
The chord is changing. Almost
a tale by Brothers Grimm: how items
at the stroke of three are one,
and once alone, the floor's warping.

THE SUN IS A PRIEST OF SORTS

Light, even with our damaged ozone layer
making your ultra-violet rays dangerous,
proves a constant from your boiling self,
who is a priest of sorts, fission and fusion
mediating sacraments of sorts, and almost
undoing me to substitute cells of light.

Like Juan de la Cruz, I will it now,
if this light overshadow me, to be done
accordingly, even if hidden from me, or by
my own twisting and turning to avoid you,
done now, and with abandon you take me.
I stand ready among the antlers of fallen trees.

You are the wounded, yet healing source
reported as both particle and wave.
Your signature is paradox in passing,
Kilroy-was-here graffiti. Deep the heat of you.
Some surprise, as she threw the *I Ching*
and "Shock" was followed by "Follow."

Even the discovery of a Celtic cauldron
utters your benediction, just imagining
the workmanship. At least four silver smiths
in the Iron Age were needed to finish it,
the bellows and the sparks, exactly so,
in the firmament and below, preside.

ENCHANTED PROPERTY

Ants, chinch bugs, fungus and weeds beware.
Your monarch beats a path to your ugly door.
I bring your tax reassessment and your worst subpoena
and leave your mailbox tortured for information.
Alas, why not we just collect each other, I keep thinking.
But I know the creatures of my back yard. We think
alike. We both take to our feet at the approach of
arbitration, reluctant conservationists, we,
unimpressed by the elegance of color-threaded wings.
But admit it. We have lain together by mutual consent,
held the wing of each other's back, blessing fecundity,
wrapped ourselves cocoon-like, found akimbo at dawn.
Now she can barely endure me. So I give her hives
and at night she suffers the itching rot of her legs.
Listen intently for the fall of the other shoe.
Or is that your monarch falling over the back porch?
The long drink of our description is printed and pinned.
It would be thus even if I fell like a meteor
and found the desert tribes worshiping my carcass,
even if I only walked this boundary dreaming up lines,
stopping to fix the image of enchanted property.

ALPHABET SOUP

Last night I thought of something I could say.
It involved the way your hips revolve, invitation
to encode a fine point and decode a ragged line.
I thought it possible to make a maze in which to
trap your memory, some lyric so circumspect that tea
would be forgot by Einstein, something more elaborate
than the lily of bold exposure you do so well.
Albert and I stand up for this digital world.
Approximations do not dismay us. When precision fails
we are happy to slurp your alphabet soup.

CHERISHED NOTIONS

I know better than to strike deals with Mr. Forever
or to lend out the Oyster Twins for parties.
I draw the line at sending out laundry or taking it in.
My careless way of napping is not lack of concern.
It's my way of emerging fresh to heraldry, still
maestro of curiosity, but wise to the Gnostic scams.
How about the one where hidden in the Vatican vaults
there's proof Christ espoused a postmodern plastic doll?
As if our cherished notions could dictate truth.
No reason to panic. There is a clasp that unfastens
all cherished notions, and blessed are they
who make orbit on the first or second try.

SHE IS DANISH

She is Danish. The sun rises on black coffee
as the icon of handmaiden takes your order.
You remember Copenhagen, the hanging gardens
stretching to infinity, and Hamlet's castle
outside the train window perched cliff-side
like Poe's delirium come true.
And if he's really still there, by now
he's lost the function of involuntary organs.
They have him on oxygen for the duration.
You remember how the train decoupled there. . .
She appears, Danish Eucharist to Dante.

THE ROPE IN THE CLOSET

The rope in the closet is knotted once, that fist
Genet would clench, one end frazzled like a tutu
and the other tied to 60-watt interrogation. Forgive me.
This criminal mind is counting on blacker deeds than this.
I dread most being exposed as an idealist (in both meanings),
like another Mayakovsky, head shaved, mounting ramparts.
I would rather smell deceit everywhere, and everywhere
make it my informer. I'd rather end up another Luther,
constipated and scrupulous, fastidious unto disgust,
degrees and collars and hems forever justifying nothing much.
My clock is stopped. I seem to be walking like a duck.
I have this plan to fly low into my familiar pond
and kiss the neck of incredulity daily. Forgive me.
Gertrude Stein warned me I would have days like this.

THE DIFFICULTY OF THREE DIMENSIONS

Abject slaves parade through the garden outside:
the plumber, the digger of trenches, the frantic
supervisor and his red ink. Vishnu, more like a
couch potato than a fiery pillar, positions himself
for the final solution. If I could prove Howard Hughes
slept here then maybe I'd bank on golden eggs.
Maybe I could give tours having grown my nails to claws,
seize on the headline "Impostor Murders From Iron Lung."
That's it. His off shore drilling has made our gift for gab
obsolete. Is that the meter maid yanking your regulator?
This was not the plan. But conversation stoppers also serve.
All three dimensions beg for identity, even a Mescal worm
or peeping Toms. Best to call the tribunal on my cunning horn.
The blood of sculpture is mine. Who needs curtains.
The neighbors may as well know we're mostly perpendicular.
Vishnu for all the world keeps planning around his consort,
belly up and languid in his quilt, bitter herbs on standby.

IT WAS YOUR PATRICIAN LIPS

It was your patrician lips that gave you away
and made me your slave. Events are unimportant.
It's the curve of your spine that entices.
Appendages muster some truncated tribute.
Flashes atop your broadcast tower
warns stray advances to veer sharply.
The knuckles of your back deserve devotion
expected from cathedral scholarship finally
touching the threshold of St. Lazarus.
Everywhere the genius of flying buttresses,
the sanctuary roof and the deafening bells,
outlined hips and thighs, studied candor
braced for all the world to see how I beg
secretly for your professorship near my tabernacle.

SLEDDING SEAWARD

The flip of the coin answers to no one. It arrives
with the simplicity of a pelican sledding seaward.
It prances without legs to kitchen duty, all tail and
conscience to meet its fate: incubation or consumption.
It could have been something overheard that undermined.
It could have been our patch of green, those picnic dreams
that spent us like money spends all faith in pockets:
there beside the canal, Alamo carnage fresh, I Parisian dude
by Cézanne and you so Parisian nude. It could have been
my gross neglect, the first mistake worming Adam's apple,
or some species of justice poking through the divine canvas.
How could I blame that thatch of ground you call south,
and I call north? We both forgot the question once too often.

HE ASKED TO BE KNOWN

He asked to be known for his decisive moment,
the moment which began with breaking up furniture
to build the fire of hospitality, an old cradle,
its spokes the perfect kindling, all collapsed
and blazing in his Renaissance hearth. The flames
exclaimed inferno when the cardboard box was added.
They licked outside the definition of grate into
the intimacy of household for something flammable.
He took a log and flung it in, pushing its source
deeper into the Middle Ages, deeper into discharge
where Aristotle ponders the bust of Homer, deeper
into stoic ancestors willing to be ash for warmth.
He asked to be known for this, and not for the bouncing
of checks, the singing for supper, or the walking home.

MINE UMBRA

Enter mine umbra that blots out light for me, my fault,
and she whose Tantric faith excludes my hope for light.
She points out the genocide of Caananites and Jebusites
by agents of my jealous god's conquest for milk and honey.
I make her brood on nobler times, alleged Amazons
who amputated one breast to better draw the bow.
I see myself thrashing through a swamp
as sirens blare and baying hounds are closing in.
Somehow I reach those pillars of classical aspiration
where buddies offer stogies and brandy and happy lies.
Truth is, I have met the migrant living in my field,
and I am he, posing with machete like Ché himself.
She recalls fondly a Rosicrucian pyramid, and blazoned
on the far wall the single word: "TRY."
But I am no Hapsburg to unite the warring mobs
under my dynastic banner, nor a slave to Amazons.
I'm doing well to have stood up to my mother
when she claimed she could see my tragic flaw.

THE NIGHT MY METAPHORS TOOK ME FOR ANALYSIS

I had been staring at the tile kitchen counter
with toy cars and the android sculpture,
and the lights being low, I could imagine a lake.

It was the haunted ebony lake where votive barges
are poling to a recondite chant without torches.
It was a lake where Darwin once whispered "Eureka,"

the sort of place one's analyst dreams of hearing.
The urge to free associate took over:
". . . lake, swim, moon, spoon, silver, gold, the Olympics,

the grand career of Johnny Weissmuller . . ."
And his body, dare we say it, was Gerber fed
and hairless and totally derivative, just like

Tarzan would have to be, a man recreated
from the ribs of our own enlightened fables,
Rousseau's science experiment gone viral.

FINDING LONGITUDE

It is an ambitious project.
From my vantage point at prime meridian
the puzzle was less daunting.

I turned a blind eye on the stars
proven useless to the Oedipus Rex
and drew an arbitrary vertical line

from Jocasta's scalp to her pubic bone.
Now it became a matter of counting,
like notes played against the metronome.

But I am still far from practical solution.
The wreckage of craft without longitude
haunts me, those victims strangling on brine

paralyze my will, tempt me to connect the dots
or leave to fate our true course.
Better to hug the shore and rely on dead reckoning

like academy judges dismissing the nonobjective.
Or we could read the entrails of chickens
before each launch and look for omens.

Who am I to invent time zones?
Who appointed me Archimedes of the globe?
Newton was summoned to Parliament

to testify before a select committee
regarding the lack of longitude.
He recommended a contest with a prize

that would drive the best minds to solution.
I have already gambled for the seamless robe.
Soon I will pierce the heart of naked truth.

RUBBER BAT

The boy pulls a rubber bat across the floor on a string
as "Wild Kingdom" documents by video exotic varieties
of sight and hearing by creatures: multiplex vision
of ants, the nuanced whining of dolphins, all picked up
and renown by the blind instruments that human minds
devised for seeing and hearing. The boy finds the decibel
within his throat that speaks equally to life organic
and life angelic. He starts to swing the bat above
his head, begins the orbit that seeks the stratosphere
of Titans and Roman gods, insists with classical candor
that nature's laws must imitate the mind's keen passion
for hierarchy. He drones the liturgy of egg and sporadic
sperm blindly colliding, yet like no meteor that scars
at random but rather brings to all things the seeing,
hearing, and knowing that no separate stone can speak of.

TADPOLES

"Tadpoles, eyes bulging, can barely find their way . . ."
She reads to him of his beloved natural wonders,
every detail of the process as fascinating as any story.
He stops her to argue the theory of gravitational forces.
He daily makes replicas of crustaceans with his flexi-blocks
and his favorite Christmas gift was a dinosaur skeleton
you wind up, and it walks, inching as if heading upstream
where spawning and dying lay down together.
Yesterday he identified the slide into the next epoch.
It was the moment of seeing the great blue heron
winging out of the creek, almost weary, lugging its
magnificent blueness and beak and scrawny legs.
Seeing this, we both knew the hunger for information
from now on would be the guiding spirit of our world.

SECRETS OF THE VENUS FLY TRAP

The story of this carnivorous plant begins with its trap
boldly outstretched, inviting, welcoming, offering premium
insect real estate with a view of the cabbage patch.
Buggy landings trigger the toothy jaws to close. Strike one
if the victim is indigestible. Without the creature's struggle
or an outside hand causing artificial stimulation, fly trap
will not press its mitt air tight and release its bile that must
absorb the inner tissues through the bug's exoskeleton.
Strike two if you feed it hamburger and forget to massage.
The plant will rot from bacteria and never seal tight.
But baseball history was made when Cool Arm Luke
pitched in a seed of wheat, massaged as directed,
and six days later the seed had sprouted inside fly trap's mouth.
On the seventh he rested, the manual now useless.

MEADOWLANDS TELECAST

1

In the fifth race, Sustained Tranquility, a long shot.
Our lot, to spit masticated pigment on psychic cave walls
to even the odds. So pretty, positively aquiline,
those Neolithic profiles in full gallop, bent on terminus,
obscured by this photo-finish replayed on the monitors.
Here we seem to remember our origins as scavengers,
back before the knees would lock or the thumb plumb.
Here the first joy, finding the carcass picked clean
and taking sloppy seconds in the smashing of bones
and the picking for the marrow, is almost genteel.
Sustained Tranquility. You would think you'd thank your
lucky stars she crossed your path. If only now you
could change that channel, lace her feed. . . "They're off!"

2

"Scale The Wall on the outside. . ." Toulouse sketches
from his high stool while hooves silently pound.
"Sweet, sweet" muses aloud the the fat, indigent
presumption descending the chrome and marble staircase.
The probable favorites wag at the Meadowlands.

The proper study of racing sheets flaps. Civilized
at last, we agree to waltz on to what fate decrees.
Alone. The forest is turnpiked in G-strings. Fast.
"Absolute Grief on the inside. . ." Toulouse kicks
with short legs the ribs of no horse. Harlot Remembered
passes on the outside like a peek through lace no
man of science could resist. A sure thing in the tenth.
Her assembled suitors are like Rembrandt's Night Watch.

3

Two days of speculation later, as the bond market swooped
in a correction leaving your vision of boom times doubtful,
you went back to the well of your doom to sell cheap.
The whole thing can be graphed. The system is foolproof.
You mix the earth's pigments with your saliva, you chew
with the same jaws that will leave clues of your obsession,
and you blow in bursts on any available wall of instruction.
Soon you will have students who can decode and apply it.
They will gather with eyes riveted in different directions,
but each following the same racing forms, each race
a potential score, each intuition respected instantly.
Your attention, ladies and gentlemen. These creatures
at which we glance over have finally come full circle.

TARZAN THE APE MAN

Tarzan was first encountered on screen
as nearly mute curiosity
and ferocious instinct for mating
encountering an expedition in search
of the fabled elephant's bone yard.
Hapless "poor devil" extras fall
from the legendary escarpment
sheltering the hidden valley
where the mighty mammal, perhaps nature
itself, is said to go to die like galaxies
groping their way to the next Black Hole.
Jane was first encountered seduced by Tarzan,
her refinement shattered by his version of paradise,
a new refinement coaxed from his hollowed tree.
The boneyard pilgrimage continued.
The ape man is sucked into Jane's family problems.
He takes on the role of rescuer
and battles a monster in a pit
while Jolson pygmies rampage
and elephants stampede to his cry
for one more day of elephant glory.

Our last glimpse of the star-crossed couple,
is them waving happily to 1950 America,
having given short shrift to their classic
water play that finally opened her female being
to his being demonstrably male.

YOUR CARD COMMEMORATING MY BIRTHDAY

Your card commemorating my birthday arrived.
The undersea of whales and dolphins sings
to a blistering Tintoretto sunset, yin and yang
doing its mystic dance.
It's a classy card. You are a classy woman,
I give you that, I always gave you that.
I even like the Emersonian restraint
of your wish for me to manifest
my aspirations and my dreams, to manifest,
with warm regards impressively liturgical,
your name reading as "Amen" across the page.
You are a true Transcendentalist.
I gave you that, I'll always give you that.
I might, even if here we could reconcile,
sabotage everything by taking issue with "manifest."
It had seemed to me I had *been* manifesting.
I suppose on judgment day, you and I
will be gouging out each other's eyes,
at St. Peter's utter dismay, over our
worse than Romeo's miscarried communiqués.

But your wish for my dreams and aspirations
I genuinely accept with gratitude,
that one so devout still prays for me . . .

GUAM'S BROWN TREE SNAKE

We saw its face in a shell washed up on Sea Girt beach.
It was nothing supernatural. It could be patriotic, really,
when you consider the "Don't Tread On Me" motto, or
the last words of that farmer, "If left to you, this land
would remain a desert . . ." just before Geronimo shot him.

Rather than asking for the real snake to please stand up, we
assumed the crawl that blights worlds, we who hunted
with blind rapacity even that which can never be swallowed,
insinuated ourselves toward species extinction and blackouts . . .
From this sea to shining sea, someone's Bronco inches north.

We improvised that look in the eye of all reptiles, that single
first directive targeted for lunar touchdown, at great cost
and despite total ignorance of code 1202: paydirt.
This is not the face of Venus sliding modestly into Venice.
This is the necrotizing aphasia of Guam's brown tree snake.

It stuns first with its eyes. It adores this transaction,
but strikes regardless, prefers there be no boundary between
its stomach and your alleged autonomy, would exemplify
your "not this, not this . . ." the swamis call discernment,
fetal individuations running backward to oblivion . . .

Its appetite extends to signatures on a random seashell.
It would have us silenced, would be so even if bureaucrats
never existed. Nature would eventually produce the one thing
that can never be satisfied and never be destroyed,
too stupid to destroy itself and too deadly to be ignored.

It snatches children from their mothers! I'll be the mother here!
I propose we analyze this zombie in our midst. No safety in trees.
It *must* favor something to its demise, some carrot/ garrote
combination, unless it is boundlessly closed to temptations.
Its habits *must* embrace more than itself, indifferent oneness

inhabiting everything everywhere like one-world governance.
Have we lost sight of the miracle of republics? Are we fodder?
If this thing is alien, why are we marching on Leningrad?
Its spawn of crippled history is founding diseased colonies.
Will we finally die in the snow with all other besieging armies?

THIS BUSINESS OF BECOMING TYPICAL

It happened by increments, this business of becoming typical,
this unsuspected drift to middle age stereotype from the lofty
Olympian avant garde you once thought yourself. Your life
you thought was like a wild preserve, a jungle that even to its
keeper had grown unfathomable with each species mutating
as conditions and climate changed, is, in truth, more like
a private magisterium preserving doctrines, another in the long
succession of men over forty with fun complaints that anyone
under thirty has heard before, like the priest in his tedious box.
Obliterating genus, natural selection marches on.
Predictably, ambition is the target of its mounting pogroms.
But while the clerks of license have you tar baby trapped in
hapless loss, you still plead for anything but the briar patch.

PSYCHIC DIGESTION

The brain is a kind of worm, a flaccid tube
conducting its world slowly through its body,
encoding and decoding with primordial appetite,
invisibly honeycombing the ground we stand on
and finally leaving fossil prints for renewed
psychic digestion. The brain is my uncircumcised
and creeping alien self, finally feeding on itself
when stranded in orbit, obsessing on loss, frantic
before the great heel of Genesis crushes me.

INCOGNITO

It first appeared under my glass incognito.
It browsed or stampeded like any dumb victim
or like a child in a Gothic library killing time
with no pattern beyond some eternal regression of
causes outside itself (like any other species).
This man of science was seduced by nature's chain.
I saw only the grand schema and overlooked the curse,
the wanting it all both ways and no strings attached
side-stepping the scavenger. I saw only the order of
pecking on the flip chart, missing it until I noted:
it alone maintains its marrow in death, it alone
leaves evidence of memories stacked in such manner as
to move time forward . . . and Olé! There it was,
horns swinging, isolated from its field,
on the head of my pin: the curse from which cases spring!
Now I preach the merit of televised gossip.
I recommend the practice of en masse scrutiny of
things pitiful, a beast infested annoyingly by
parasites and equally annoying birds of grooming,
chained to the sky of some grace parceled too late.

PANEGYRIC IDEATION

The sound was a kind of splatter,
those round assured Caucasian sounds
of Roman rubrics marching the downbeat,
three claps to each quatro meter
leaving ample room for African insouciance.
Improvisation was Dada's first lesson.
The second, becoming sculpture when necessary.
It is those times we turn to pillars of salt
(or such) that maybe, drums syncopating,
Mucho Gusto gives herself in secret,
working herself upbeat into Augustan feet.
They worked it like the "Killing the Calf" gag
till Cromwell finished off England's rood.
It ended with the plaintive sax angling
that last percipience, Tudor ended,
things empirical biting and thrashing
on the hook of thinking fast.

The mendacity of the world manages
to hold sway despite all sedulous editing.

Things Neo-Classical had melted into the Hellespont
and emerged wearing the green jacket that terrorized
Sir Gawain. Romanticism. Without doubt, sincerity
deserves at least one last cast into earned ambivalence.

The sublime was born thus: twilight urination
in shadowy Gethsemane, pale moon punctuation.

THE NECESSITY OF LEARNING FRENCH

One could involuntarily resist learning a language
as casual and freely mumbled as French.
The "Marseillaise," with its rousing deconstruction,
wins the first place on the charts. Undertow and mayhem
crowns the pauper and lobs the Crown. Lingua
Saturnalia is subwayed and ground to a paste.
Paranoia proven lyrical pronounced backwards says it all.
Nothing less will do, and one is forced to admit
the necessity of learning French.

One could resist learning a language, but be also
enchanted by its gift for the slurred twist, the candid
obliquity, the sheer artifice of triumph, like botanists'
just reported amazing genetic engineering feat:
a plant that produces plastic. Someone went down
on basic aroused humors for this one,
was not ashamed to let tongue disorder the senses
to bring out the pearl of speaking French.
This just in: satellite proof, the Big Bang
graduates from theory to fact.

AMPUTATED FINGERS

It was a gesture that truly broadened into a subject.
Few people realize that dismemberment has often been
history's fondest tribute, like Galileo's finger

still pointing star-ward, or that finger of Descartes
that penned the words "*Cogito, ergo sum*" enshrined
like martyrs' revered amputated parts all scattered

throughout that cyclopean Europe, consecrating altars.
It's a fact that the grandfather century, Age of Reason,
preserved countless human fingers in countless jars

and clockwork inventiveness was in fact a wonder,
and invited surprising craft to glorify things decadent.
It was not just the age of reason, but of touch.

The senses, and all their secrets, found a playmate
in this imagination that now walks abroad, free standing,
looking vulnerable as Firenze's "David," with eye

and arm cocked, taking measure and counting odds.
Our Titan parents are the senses and the imagination
now mating into being our future pantheon, digital Olympus.

The ultimate subject that emerges will doubtless be green
and shaped more like the profile of old Osiris, then off
to Mt. Carmel to feed like a cursor across the screen.

THE SPIRIT OF THE STAIRCASE

Roundly sprung, the bibliographical display
floor to ceiling for three stories, the multiple
staircase views offer oneself moving downward,

blithely and in Futurist accord down, and down again.
One lands in a faculty chat: how false analogies
thrive in the hothouse of fine distinctions (good news)

and that deconstruction will probably save us
if it's not too late (more good news). Then it occurs
to interject a dinosaur of subjectivity, one that lunges

perversely, an unexpected horn growing from its
metonymic head, so beyond postmodern it's classical.
One thinks better of it. The tar pit is crowded,

and shouting "Plus Ultra" would cause panic.
Mind's eye may yet pull out extant
that which could be, saved by Hollywood

with all its impact of blunt objects well placed.
The odds for divining rods advancing literature are poor.
This is disembodied flotsam owing nothing to no one.

THE THEORY THAT MAN DESCENDED FROM BIRD

It was a fleeting glimpse at first.
This year it became a religion.
It began as an urge to grub

for unsavory facts, and now I flock
to the conference that won Chaucer,
my Canterbury tail twitching.

No coincidence, white dove descending.
Consider the unforgivable sin.
Dire consequences await the traitor

to the hollow bones and sharp beak
and flitting eyes. We owe him
our best features . . . Or is it her?

I owe the bird my fondness for vestments,
and have stood me like a presidential seal.
If only I were bald enough to pull it off.

The birds have the venerable mugs
of my grandparents. I see too much in this?
My face stares back with incredulity.

Ancestors had played the fool that I
might someday join with their darting
in crooked lines with straight conclusions.

TONGUE IN CHOICE AT THE MET

I am probably the incubus that could rob her sleep.
I am same spider in the corner there, dangling
and then up into rafters to wait,
saving a permanent doubt

        to desiccate that once saved

        always smug demeanor.

I, you see, cannot imagine God without that fabulous helmet
that she so Calvinistically dismissed.

        Barely visible in the margin

        this tiny Creator Face

        radiates the central drama

        here at the River Jordan.

That face, especially the helmet, will guarantee
no block of cheese will be widely worshiped instead.
Item: That confused and dappled hermit lying in his forest.
Ah, the flanks of near invisible deer.
Beyond any hopes of design he stares
with ferocious longing forever unlike all else
grazing or buzzing or waving all around him,
collapsed in compost, blending with incognition,
forever a tongue in choice.

What here, surreal narrative,

young women aroused by pageantry,

nude among marble institutions,

absorbed in nocturnal libations

and systematic ritual offerings

in free spirited poses.

"This is neither the time nor the place"

I told her is the inscription I want for by head stone.

She clutched my arm like General Joan to her chief-of-staff,

and I wanted to clutch her by the hair

and inject the antidote, instill the rapture,

dissuade from all campaigns devoid of oscillating vision.

RELICS

There is nothing pagan in the fetish for relics.
The bones of a mascot tutelary spirit, its feathers
and beneath all its microbes in that miasmic soup

washing monstrous, stranded Nile creatures ashore . . .
Even the sacred spots where The Hawk touched ground,
these are not as pagan as they seem. They are relics

because sacramentals take many shapes, and always honor
the proximity of the beloved, honors it with specificity
of form and matter, prepared to itemize her attributes

unabashed as a candidate for office, eager to prize
anything she has touched, anything that strikes her wonderful,
anything suffered deserving my vigil or pilgrimage

to find at last the great mystery waiting in the ordinary.
Relics are an honoring of each discreet memory of love:
phantom Romeos, ex-husbands, you, prepared to wear horns

right down to the staging of the historic debates.
It is faith, not appeasement, this sentimental gesture
of taking pride in her labyrinthine generosity of soul.

IF I WRITE YOU A POEM WILL YOU DANCE ON MY TABLE

Crustacean on vacation sporting
metaphorical shell and claws
meets a naked oyster in a bar.
She offers him a fulcrum and a spot
to stand to watch her pearl emerge,
the tiny orb that earned for her
the menu headline. How Genesis!
Like cherubim descending on brutes
she parachutes, an undulating cloud.
Oh sad miscalculation, knowing not
he only just absolved himself
while crawling out from muck to feed
on shame. Gabrielle, he cannot bear
to handle what he can't consume unless
he fooled himself to thinking that
his money is a robot on your moon.

BIRD MIGRATIONS

Emerging from the boreal Canadian forests,
they ride the Appalachian ridges for maybe Argentina.
They belong to the same club, like those courtiers
in Urbino who refined the virtues of conversation.
Star maps will scan within precise faculties.
Renaissance of birds. Just so did Urbino find London,
the snowy owls conferring: "What is it that all women want?"
They are said to erupt in a blinding penumbra
and wink not on the royal note that is unified flux.

STILL PICKING PEAS

I have long performed for such as these, drunks
without a taste for avant garde, throwing back my line:
"What are you, man of science or science experiment?"
That one startled me. It put me on the defense.
The audience, as per Aquinas, is genus unto itself,
a single angel differing from another as species differ.
Fallen angel, this audience, heckled me, fingers
still picking peas in its automatic wretchedness.
I summoned my retort: "Demonstrable!" I said.
The audience was thrashing in foliage beyond
a silence like a wall of gigantic stones, and pouncing
at last it had me by its claws. "Harry Houdini?"
"Why yes," I said. "And you, I presume, are Cursed Luck.
Let me introduce you to my friend Science Experiment."

I WATCH THE CANTOR FOR MY CUE

A prophecy will be fulfilled within their hearing.
It will either prove Freud's point or it won't,
how exposure of repression proves the royal road to sanity,
how wisdom requires someone's permission to be cheerful.
Something is at stake here for this dubious crowd.
I'm in a synagogue. I watch the cantor for my cue.
He begins the majestic petition. Soon they will make book
on my catechism, run me out of town, and spread rumors:
"He trapped evil spirits in swine and ran the herd off a cliff."

SONG SPIEL

Me thought Mack the Knife had visited
at the horned gate, puns notwithstanding,
and struck a skeptical Rabelaisian pose.
Someone distinguished false from true dreams
showing respect for "rêve étoilé," for transports
and prophetic presences. I considered sleep.
I considered drama, and archeologists showed me
the ivory neck of Shulamite found among tusks
and philanderers in quadrant 5 of the dig.
The fragments found here are pieced together
as songs of praise, not drama, which the priests
monopolize in their seasonal cultic enactments
and never leave their fragments unconsumed.
Me thought these songs could be staged effectively,
that a reconstruction of the circumcision scene
would play well against the modern preference
for quotidian cunning, unambiguous transparent horn.

IF I COULD READ PALMS

If I could read palms I think I would.
I have been ridiculed for discipleship
in foot massage for healthier interior organs.
Equally, the "reflexology" of palms furthers.
Why not read them? Have they not
stemmed the tide of anthropoid body hair?
In my right hand I see a message from
a dying Roland to his absent troops.
You will meet a crisis, it says, and you
will have nothing to hold. The meaning will
come clear, how each line is earned, too late.
Candidate for positive affirmations? Maybe.
But the millions climbing on bare knees
to see the miraculous portrait are not,
to me, an episode of *Believe It Or Not.*
Some of my best friends have climbed steps
on bleeding knees. There is no superstition
I would not enlist to dispel the rumor
that religion is only for the weak.

TODAY

It can happen anywhere,
your under-used under-self blooming
so a glimpse in this breeze
tells all we need know.

Last night the world ended.
It made all the canonized signs:
lightning, MGM sky, ominous wind.
God was pulling his punches again.

So it ended, like any good opera,
a travesty preordained,
predicted by a chorus line of gypsies.
No deluge exactly . . .

So it began, soft as a baby's head
or a sandwich too big to bite.
New inclinations in the perennial soil
are following instructions to the letter.

WATCHING WITH INTEREST

My Chaucerian pilgrimage seems complete, with only the final
disclaimer left to say and the final day to call my rival.
I feel my blades on ice. She leans into my center, and I know
with Sibylline cognition that secretions meant for me
have begun inside where she needs me most, her life itself
in my hands, my Lewis and Clark, my CIA hands.
She makes me touch her spheres of influence, she invites
a shameless hegemony with those eyes like Portia's portrait.
She has come to save my pound of flesh. She takes my case.
She has hovered with infinite mercy on the flesh in question,
lingered over it with speeches, caresses, even begged for it.
If the jury is hung, I can say at least they watch with interest.

A SINGLE PEARL

I

The line deletes . . . shows bold as a Buddha on skates
and then vanishes, cradled by digits one moment and Nirvana
the next, pedagogical on Tuesday and esoteric by Thursday . . .
deletes, and Renoir's party comes alive.
UFOs sail the first day of autumn and earthlings are planning
for Guy Fawkes Day. Vacuum cleaner rouses prehistorically and flies
like a DC7 hunted by bomb threats from a Columbian cartel,
haunting the carpet landscape of chaos and seeds of chaos,
for wreckage and signs of life, for statistics on risk factors
and danger of perfect union, the perfect tool
matching the perfect skill.

The perfect fool holds the door for Grendel and checks his coat.
Beowulf is miles away, hoisting sail for world peace or grand merger.
You will be facing your own casualty.
Hammer and sickle will start to make sense.
Nuclear bombs will be proven clearly necessary . . .
not contingent on malice, just inevitable, preordained,
a criminal visitation made epic.

Chamberlain flickers on the documentary, so optimistic,
so confident you won't end up bleeding in your own bed.
Dawn is the most terrible time, the bodies littered
and unexploded shells buried in the plush upholstery.

I post myself guard at the patio door overseeing the back fence.
The story of Gulliver whipped by Lilliputians comes to mind,
and my mission: to think small, to visualize angels
waltzing with bacteria on the head of a pin . . . lobotomized sentry
planning to dust for anomalies, clues, coded messages. . .
I have made inventory. My hair and limbs are tacked down.
My faith in mathematics is shaken; the function of zero gives pause
and infinity the last laugh. I am Sherlock to debauched lingerie
and scented scarves with strange stains.
Transients make those winks. . .
They are still lurking at the Laundromat, sharpening something.

Alien footprints have infested this house . . .
        They reproduce crazily
like paramecium. I am their naturalist.
        I can read the phalanx of toes
and the Mount of Saturn,
        have classified their osmotic organs and habits . . .

But all the while I dream of the Alezar Library,
   discussion hot
on Newton's Law and when to expect
   the Twelfth Imam, where public
prayer is forehead lowered and stamped by the ground.
   I have my research
to comfort my dotage. Instead of wisdom,
   my yield will be senility.
Uncomprehending this record of unseen invasion,
   my children will recite:
". . . as if you live forever . . .as if you die tomorrow . . .,"
   the book
come home to nest among fossils and wormwood,
   the binding broken.

By now I could be finishing up
   my last of eighty-nine stone faces
on Easter Island, the world's navel,
   carving them directly from cliffs
and mounting them like satellite dishes
   with detached eyes facing inland
so the sea and wind become their body,
   inland to glare at a desert once a paradise . . .

By now I could be taking that small step for a man
        onto lunar surfaces, scratching the birdman sign
into sheer rock and looking back through my visor,
        the earth's light carving me
as neatly as cheese into something to bless fertility.
        I will soon be listening to the old woman's song
through her cat's cradle, the last memory of past glory
        reduced to nursery rhymes and platitudes.

II

I could just imagine it, as if your star chart threaded
unseen quasars for my meteorite embattled Voyager.
This river you love loves you back. It counsels in Druid
granite, composes driftwood I imagine your legend beheld . . .
Our souls trudge light-years ahead of us, unleashing hope
like playful dogs leaping towards us along the river trail,
Buddha-nature with muddy feet and tongues lolling.
Somewhere in the constellation Corvus, one-eyed physicists
are tenderly smashing the atom. Somewhere in those rapids
Pisces struggles upstream with a single pearl in its belly.

The Fisher King lives upstream. He is my brother-in-law,
venerated by Karl Sterner and Ken Delahunty. Gerry Stern
in combat boots was confirmed as poet in that house, and I
have filled my cup there more than once. His location hangs
in a pocket, unnoticed by traffic on route 32 or 611 . . .
Scholars yet unborn are hovering like the blue heron to
reconstruct or speculate upon the facts, convinced the Grail
was buried near the blood pit in the grotto. On Valentine's Day
his wife, my sister, welcomes Parcival to feast on pasta and
waits for the "Hng!" that would spiral to the skylight overhead.

Meanwhile, back where Cronus languishes on the second floor,
shouts are heard from the wallpaper: "Before the portals of the
cold place, the horns of light shall be burning!" Nine damsels
contemplate with Pre-Raphaelite marvel the Raven in his catatonia.
These walls are a trail of potent flowers stacked to the ceiling
where watermarks haphazard a guess as to the moon's phase.
Portraits hang amid the jungle, boys in first Communion suits:
This a young Henry James, this an Arthur Rimbaud . . .
Move quickly to the third floor and sit among the trees that scrape
their limbs on the panes. Remember to say, "No, sleep on."

This is middle-aged Edgar Rice Burroughs postulating treehouse.
This is intuition of nature's own language promulgated by epistles.
This is some kind of ideal marriage of the human and the beast,
like centaurs and griffins, the best of two worlds, and a Jane
who dreamed as a girl of squatting by rice patties,
Padma Sambhava with a tongue of fire crowning her,
ready to return again and again to the mundane hearth
to feed her little Tarzans. She is lotus born.
She had her vision of union while still in the drawing rooms,
long before she met the ape man.
This is the blazing tongue of her mouth, and this
the ignited body of the entire animal kingdom.

The Blue Heron

He rouses himself in the forest primeval. His breath is musk.
The familiar rocking of the earth and the scent of next kill. . .
Turning on the tubes, another game of Nintendo, "Zelda,"
where you finally earn the weapons for the next mysterious room,
where you nimbly defeat all darts or hidden cobras in time to
reach the monster's head and save mankind with one deadly twist.
Even then, he rears like a chimp as history's cargo washes ashore.
He will soon be dancing with the blue heron. In this version,
Tarzan pulls out the plug. This one has him cradled in moon craters,
feeding on lovers' mutterings 200,000 miles away,
and music somehow.

III

What drains out first is memory.

    He knuckles the music box on her porcelain,

shares her soap, the many hairs

    married in tallow, and unchains her Isis

searching for body parts. Pulsating

    shower head . . . These relics, even those

of foreign gods, shine like the burning bush.

    These, the feathers you say

you wore at Marti Gras, bed sheet Amazon's

    saucy ballet now midwinter

night's dream . . . "She nearly caused a riot"

    must have been the headlines.

They only saw the iceberg's tip.

    I can see the whole continental drift,

the fossil exposure along the floor,

    the crawling compulsion with pen

in hand to make the possible eruption

    necessary. Only you know the secret

landings along the canal where

    sprites and indigenous creatures frolic . . .

. . . know the cords strung on spinal ridges

    now anointed for my dying.

O chaste and melancholy song,

    she shows me perfect mercy here.

She will be remembered ever after for these lavish oils

    and first words:

"Where did *you* come from?" I will live

    until her candor orbits earth.

Scenes from the washing of feet

    had emerged from the walls like

Placido's tenor, like bas relief depicting

    prophets wrestling and virgins

praying, and I, your offering in aromatic

    unction, was prone on your

altar, some Prufrock become the Sistine Adam

    as you lifted my arm

and pointed my finger, and I swore

    my judgment is no more than Zen

and my appetite no less than the Baptist ravenous for locusts.

Later we discussed Madam Blavatsky
      and the cards reversed, "Death"
in particular. You told of the totem
      that drove you to the sweat lodge.

Gurdjieff is your great grand uncle
      posed here with snakes in his hair,
and here the souvenir of first friendship.
      Your memories kept me
blessedly empty, a hollow reed
      for either Pan or Holy Ghost to pipe.
Her melody lingered in the highlight patterns bursting through
where least expected,
      when her divine fingering on trembling skin
kept me filled with that invisible nectar she'd asked me to see,
to visualize her honey flow, inexorable as lava,
      slow and blistering
to the poisons of world pretensions,
      moving through me at a touch.

As it rains pennies from heaven,
      those critters who kiss and bite
are pairing and nesting,
      and Lenten photosynthesis yields ashes with air.

Lambertville utters bell-like
      and buds ignore the frost, and puddles pond
while this visitor's feet plod.
      My feet had scraped off mud before landing
and my steps wound up to your dormers
      to Futon sublimity. First
I embrace you as comrade in the body,
      still trapped in physiology.
Lymphatic system, for example. You are worth an epic,
      node clusters
tributaried body wide, shades of Troy
      blazing after too much horseplay.
Second, I embrace you as sanctuary,
      riblike sky nest with no trap doors.
The flies pinball on the panes and whine their fathomless dirge.

It flows by, this dark light into souls,
      this Delaware River, mumbling
fearful pillow talk of campaigns in peril
      and hopes soon dashed,
General George whispering to Martha
      and pleading with Congress.
My Martha sees only the rescue of
      Tibet and its recondite sacraments.

I see only Hessians closing on
      my tattered ranks, impending pillory.
We plan from separate screens
      with different 3-D glasses, beyond
conventional properties of intimacy,
      delivering distance conceptualized.
For now, we measure our steps
      and compose classification contracts.
But the great and terrible day is coming
      when human contracts shred.
Only our darkest lights will put together Humpty world
      on D-Day.

IV

A garden like Eden was reported by poets
      intact in New Jersey.
The high priestess of its central tree
      is a single parent, they say,
and the child who walks on water in Rambo gear,
      forbidden fruit
she guards for the Dalai Lama.
      In this place, the fall is not granted.
The Rambo child dictates all judgments.
      His icon is all that keeps
the serpent mesmerized and demons
      lurching at the outer gates . . .
Only he has named all beasts. Here, we do not circumcise.
      We have only to kiss the icon
of the Rambo child, wish into being
      our heart's desire, and bow
to applause for the Oscar performance
while waving good-bye to Israel's earned chapter and verse.

And even as the forsythia strangely blooms in concert
with dogwood and cherry; daffodils, azaleas and tulips
choiring their notes of color to rhythms of Delaware rapids
and there, the great blue heron rising. . . there, a circling
kite . . . she pronounced those ancient syllables: "I wish
I had never met you." It has liturgical familiarity and finality.
I silently intoned the response, "Houston, we have a problem."
Mankind's giant step defers to daffodils, azaleas and tulips
choiring their notes of color to rhythms of Delaware rapids
and there, the great blue heron rising . . . and pennies falling.

Last night I dreamed I could fly feet first and close
to the ground at incredible speed. I could steer myself
by cocking legs to left or right. I carried her image
carved from stone inside a cavity within my chest. Hired
to haul a rectangular crate from here to there, I settled
into the truck, vaguely aware that inside that crate
languished my worst nightmare. It exuded a familiar stench.
My x-ray eyes exposed the horrible truth in all its horror.
I wanted to tell her we were in danger, but my chest
cavity had grown smaller and she was facing backward.

My ordinary self awakes to portraits
      of coworkers and coffee.
My chest has no cavity,
      and her photo was removed from my wall.
Reports are due and memos abound.
      For lunch, at Dairy Queen,
those solid spots on the pavement stick to my sole,
      and I jump as Brad claims a victim to backward stepping
into careless gum.
      You would think a scorpion had bit him, he said.
This stringy clinging I scraped
      as the heat of ordinary life chanted *AUM*
and the cow cooked on the spit, and the ice cream oozed
      another sundae. On Friday
someone contemplates how foolish to think
      contemplation saves.
Nothing saves. We spend until we die.
      My father says, "So what?"

My mother says, "It's you who counts,"
      and I know it's true at the bank.

My digits tremble. I look forward to digging
   another hole for my father's
trees, to chopping at roots beneath the surface,
   to shoveling adolescent
dirt until my sweat is all I am,
   until a cavity is present in the otherwise
complacent earth. I look forward to the moment
   of choice, when I say
this is deep enough, this is the nadir of depth,
   this is the hole prophesied,
this is exactly the width to accommodate new life,
   this is I, this is my father's
will, this is my sweat whose origin is choice,
   my love itself, myself
in a pile around a hole. I look forward to the tree
   that will someday stand.
I beg for a bird to sing from living trees
   the song I know to be true . . .

V

The prize is unearthed unknown,

       sentient nest of tongueless tongues

like worms that rainfall brought to the surface,

       now crushed.

Bone of my bone, what will they think of next?

       Stone blades and

incantations for the merciless hours . . .

       This vigil yields a trove of

madness. Moon craters of the brain, I name you Delphi.

       My scrutiny

is telescopic. Asteroids have ravaged all our brains,

       but your mouth

is destined for this eye, not for seeing

       but for knowing the way Zen

knows; godlessly, soullessly, nothing for the dying

       but the cud of cows

and Gorgon's head and labyrinthine flux of world contingency,

       wishful

exit sign in neon for assembled no one to be saved by nobody.

Yet silence does nurture another self
  ignored by Freud and our mothers.

Its task is to bury the dead and to grieve as Israelites grieve,
skyward. This is no prize. It's a gift,
  this struggling of pre-verbal mind
like a tourist murdering Italian,
  like a clown with a worm between
his legs, arcing his water and missing the bowl
  and blaming the gulf
unbridged and not his aim . . . toying with
  his instruments of computation
like a graduate who fluffs the tassel hanging
  from his rear view mirror.
He knows his past is as unearned as his future.
  You have washed ashore here,
your legs in the agony of little mermaids who
  forswear the sea for
anchor in gravity. You have rescued more
  than one pirate from shipwreck.

Turnpike crows labor in the fumes
  above these toll gates.

The Blue Heron

I have exact change. My name is Nemesis,
            the unprovoked solar flare that no one fears.
See how the elevated wafer cringes, hides behind
            a fan of haze as I drop my rendering unto Caesar
into gaping basket. Watch as loaves and fishes
            are sucked in, cubist pastiche as I accelerate
and veer for the shortcut, primal bliss.
            It should take years traveling at the speed of entropy
before collision into the system I once called home,
            before I kiss its cheek,
before my assembled former selves finally rend their robes
            and send my former deeds to Golgotha,
pieces of silver tinkling . . .

In the house of exile she used to have recurring dreams,
            of nakedness
in snow and making tunnels with beach shovels
            in deep over her head.
(Aunt Clara made for the freezer,
            engine that could for the Scooter Pies.)
She'd fling her body backward
            in her Michelin kid suit making angel wings,
having nowhere else to go but down.

This printing of herself gave her ideas,
the need to carve out that fallen sky
        to make those rooms and tunnels.
(Aunt Clara made for the freezer,
        engine that could for the Scooter Pies.)
She'd sit in her under-snow world, bathed
        in blue light, sleep, pose
as a fetus on some lunar beach with an ocean
        roaring off key. Someone
fashions scales and fins for her
        and feeds her the surf's icy froth.

"Four and a half months in solitary taught me to live
        with a breach
of law and confess to bedwetting."
        You try to remember the face
of the man who gave his bone marrow to a grateful child.
        It never works,
she said. Condemned to the Archipelago,
        the sergeant major dresses you down
after formation. He takes a razor and cuts off your stripes,
        and he bleeds. . .

You had to go back and face the Four Corners,
       the panel of doctors,
four, sitting at the end of the hallway, wearing
       the whites of healing
and looking like benign Parthenon
       as their verdict made the lights go dim.
"Vagina dentata," one of them said,
       the others nodding, flashing smiles.
"Coincidentia oppositorum," you replied,
       and offered to shave your head.

VI

Yet silence does nurture another self ignored
     by even Emmanuel Kant.
Consider the guilty hooligan who chose to lie,
     smirking in the court room,
savoring the memory of your subjugation,
     fondling this fetish for power
publicly like a Mycenaean pirate, a defiant prisoner,
     and noisy at first.
He'll serve at least seven years before parole is possible;
     got 25 to 30.
A Texas penitentiary, not exactly silence,
     but a kind of nurturing by
focus, a being sewn into the thigh of Zeus
     to emerge seven years
later: Dionysus in drag and more muscles
     from lifting weights, trained
at last to fill out job applications,
     maybe duly chastened more by spatial
than by temporal constriction,
     but still preened for new vandalism.

Silence nurtures our best self knowledge, given
      the material at hand.
Silence speaks in all religions from
      Osiris to Messiah bound to wood.
"Resist not evil . . ." the hardest of all sayings,
      yet emblem capturing
fashion even on gold chains
      around thin Egyptian necks. Incarnation
is today the language of marketplace sublimity,
      numinous on telescreens,
mystery religion perfected; shamans embrace it,
      ecstatic and stuck
on dumb creation's adoration of humankind.
      All things ordinary are
benedictions, simple touch invested with power:
      oil, water, breath,
nursing child, tongues of fire,
      cooked meals and bread. Whether
buried in a tree or in accident of bread,
      incarnation saves in silence.

This other self does not have the face of Gorgon,
      nor is it sleek and cold as the Egyptian cat.

It will not happily make servitude its timeless gesture
        toward cavernous instinct,
yet enchanted to think what brute sophistication
        emerged everywhere . . .
This breed of silence is rootless, on pilgrimage,
        imaging relationship like Abraham or Moses
with portable divine presence exemplified
        by food and tools.
This other self owes nothing to the blind Furies,
·   yet hears prophecies from Celtic stones.
Words become events of mind and matter entwined.
        Silence advances with approval.
You rest your head on the breast of past and future,
        favorite guests arriving at once.

It finds wayside shrines in the most unlikely spots.
        It finds ladders littered with angels,
blossoms on a trellis and celebrated here,
        this house, the banquet prepared.
It lights a lamp for the beloved.
        Silence swells like a tide,
the fishy smell and taste of it revealed as ambrosia at last . . .
this planet, this galaxy, this microscopic drama,

this sudden nova in the brain, the intuition that mercy
　　　is the uncreated Mind blissfully penetrating the created soul.
Finally, Avalon mists settled on the memory of it.
　　　The Song of Songs the troubadour had intoned
now declaims a legend: A pebble of twenty-five tons,
　　　plucked from his shoe and tossed to the arctic bear.

Should we put on our retread kneepads and flagellate our backs
or quote the principle of choice from the witness stand?
I repeat the formula: "No, sleep on."
Is this a graceful time to die?

We lie in each other's hollows, composing frames of mind,
bodily functions churning as we decide to learn Italian.
Sir Gawain is amazed; the Green Knight carries his severed head
and rides the ranks.

The Faerie Queen brandishes the Red Dragon of Wales.
Merlin's pool is the site of countless baptisms and passage rites.
Tudor and Lancaster roses make peace,
and the Berlin Wall is a jagged canvas. Party line deletes
last instructions about a sword and a lady's invisible hand.

COINCIDENCE
BECOMES
A ROOM

COINCIDENCE BECOMES A ROOM

unwarranted

suspicions swept the floor anticipating guests

the dust became disturbed and angry

agitations of matter revealed themselves as poverty

unwarranted

agitations of finitude in otherwise divine light

demonstrated the machinations of molecules, unwarranted

and uninvited curiosity crept along the sideboards

with eight speculative legs

coincidence was breeding in the carpet

their wings without credence shed for better dying

vanity was brooding in picture frames

talk-shows were teaching the art of wit

daytime drama gave us reason to suspect the worst

unwarranted

evil in some people

manifesting in secret myopic schemes

that plague our dying with imitations of living

the modern discovery that matter itself is composed of probabilities

is true

and its implications will soon be hatching some new direction

between mutual opposites

scanning the ground with new feelers that never sleep
Jules Verne opens his eyes
cities of blind industry in multifarious lenses
indulging some starlet somewhere
buried in your gifts to her
busily you make yourself born to these things
the lifting of bread crumbs
the dragging of modern garbage
the storing of modern nectar

BOOKS HUMMED QUIETLY A TUNE

each article of familiarity has reached its verdict

you

will become another you

chosen when least expected, lamphood

pointed a frayed shade

handles and knobs observing there is no point

to holding things

clockhood of digital persuasion ground another count

pillows lounged like swine for more sleep

radiators keep a wall-side vigil along this membrane

ceilings appeal to purposeless chairs

you

will become another you

will become nothing as you, but as I, the world

the world, the world, the world, the world

you

rose to address the familiar of classical persuasion

I, you said, will die for nothing less than love

what I did I leave to you

nothing

that resembles serenity, nothing that speaks

quietly

nothing more than what I dream, and always less
than what I am
shoehood talks the only intimacy
cuphood offers the final depository
bookhood yearns to be a body

SCIENCE PRETENDS TO BE NATURE

methods are running for dear life
strategies are buried alive in the bodies of allies
grand designs hide behind false walls
unidentified rooms are moaning for mercy
and memorizing the slogans of savages
technology hikes up her skirt
science pretends to be nature
genius is mute at the celebration of independence
joy has forgotten all loyalty to purpose
tragedy remembers itself as a beached whale
while continents continue to shift
and women continue to dismiss morbid fate
things classified are facts, nothing more or less than that
what is locked away, or refugee, is humanity
nothing more or less than mankind and mistakes
meeting each other in the land of approximations
and good intentions for the purpose of procreation
in hopes of some future fidelity
some imagined release of purity in life's strangulating density

methods are stopping to rest in new countries
strategies are digging graves for our friends
grand designs have been renovated as closets for new skeletons
planets will continue to revolve without our assessments

THE CAPITOL OF DO

it could have been decay
or something like sediment in the moving parts
or some misapprehension of the order of things
was it before the did became do
or is it the Capitol of Do that stinks
like Hegel in the pocket of Descartes
"I did, therefore I do"
entropy by any other name still fouling the works
would a succession of dids in a cyclotron expose
traces of unknown do-do particles
in the signature parabolics
reserved for a mad historian
it could have been the misapprehension of placement
check the bedroom
with sheets crumpled in burial mounds
and a filing cabinet fed banana peels and last week's sandwich
roll-top desk burdened by the files of savage little clerks
prodding
petitions for production in one pile

directions to perdition in another
this pile for debts, this pile for vengeance
dirty laundry and literature are the testament of did
in this misbegotten capitol of Do

ONLY RUSSIANS LOVE THEIR COUNTRY

he said he loves his country
this American called my father said it ardently
and I said, only Russians love their country, what we
know about loving one's country
wouldn't fill the first five chapters of Exodus
what he calls country
is the abstract notion of peasanthood with dignity
the illusion of every man a czar
and he called me American
and I called myself my father's son
our personhood, he said, you
cling to it as much as I, and I said, "Russians
are persons who cling to poetry"
we met in poetry
the way Russians meet, with tears of endless loss
the *concrete* notion of peasanthood with dignity crept over us

MAGNETOSPHERE

or

How the Improbable Y-Man Chases the Impossible World

You know someone has a drinking problem
when a fist fight breaks out in the final round of Jeopardy.

~George Carlin

PART I

The Blue Heron

1

What killed them was not understanding Einstein's theory.
No one can forgive a serious contestant who doesn't know
that space shortens at the speed of light,
that time slows down, and that mass quivers
like Jell-o nailed to a post . . .
They did well enough on *The Merchant of Venice*
(where mercy plays such a memorable role,)
and geography was their strong suit, having
projected travel into orbit and sorted continents
at leisure into bite-sized Chinese puzzles.
Unconscious of grace, these contestants have grabbed
the mammoth satellite while strapped outside their shuttle,
traveling all at over 190,000 miles per hour.
At age ten, I stood at attention for the TV screen.

2

The Y-Man's visor hides blank eyes.
His armor is the romance of things protean,
of things revised, of adaptation to circumstance.
Apollonian style had emerged as Cro-Magnon thaw revealed
how hostile this world really is, and armor was invented
for the luxury of feeling something personal.

Like Columbus being Catholic, we took our atmosphere
with us, the Book of Hours standard issue and recited
by all hands into the eleventh hour of panic.
By today's perspective the sleek lines and opaque surface
loom large as the symbol of our necessary risk.
Sightings of insect-like extraterrestrials seem almost
plausible, always with bulbous, vacant eyes.

3

It's always the lower jaw that tells the tale.
This he understood only after midlife, all those years before
concentrating his brushing on the visible uppers
until he realized the archaeologists must decipher
from our lowers how we used our teeth as a third hand
indicated by the enamel worn to the nubs.
He has changed the hemisphere of his concentration.
It has dropped like the larynx drops in post-infancy,
like the testicles drop, like my name drops into unlikely
record inside unlikely electronic tracings . . .
No one can forgive a serious contestant who doesn't know
how binary all computation really is, and how death
and knowledge surely find synthesis beyond both.

4

He understood virtual reality long before cybernetics
could produce it as three-dimensional experience.
He would be inclined to single out this precognition
as mere heritage of his world. All his legends and stories
drop us into this virtuality, his intimate gardens,
his plate of experienced flavor capsulized and relished.
He will not stop until he can feel the world he makes
through his own mechanical hand, feel it with more
than memory or rote abbreviation, more than bearings
that leave any natural sense with no voice.
He declared war long ago on that deafening silence
that halos the globe and is our principal misery,
a silence borne by every microbe and always hunting.

5

I have considered the new fashion of wearing one's clothes
backward. It seems to me a suitable statement
of cross purposes, suitably hostile to convention,
a recognition that the body is surrounded by itself.
The first shaman to invent a calendar was dressed thus.
It was a favorite among prophets, conceptual vulgarity enshrined
like Duchamp would dig before the chessboard captured him.

It rings the first round, where the match of wits
is the necessary backdrop to an unseen passion
as secret as the place he finds where sleep takes charge
like the leathered and spike-heeled Baubo herself,
secret behind poker-faced reflexes and blinking lights,
overcome at the last moment by one's passing oneself . . .

6

The contestants are occupied with the business of being quizzed.
They know what it takes to get their frogs to jump.
They can spot connections where you and I mumble associations.
They get it right, or they forfeit all advantage and their opponents
snatch up points until honor itself is threatened.
In their category they will soon take off, name rivers
and treaties and ecclesial councils, and they will win
only if their bombs can be guided right into bunker doorways,
if they can play night-ball with a vengeance, call the pocket
and slap their number into the slumber of thy neighbor . . .
This is the price between buyer and seller, that market mind
that caused plague wherever we have colonized.
The root of all evil is buried deep in these Darwinian whiz kids.

7

His specialty is lying in his bed of pain and pontificating.
He is Y-Man, first discovered on the East Mound, almost fetal
and flattened; the helmet known for utterances
was planted phallic-like above the grave, which indications are
was central to all that his tribe considered numinous.
We think his hand diagramed procedures for hunting and gathering.
His words were agonized, but strangely lyrical,
often hypercritical, authoritative and yet desperate for attention,
like a brat stamping his foot and demanding program access.
His shroud is extant, a banner displayed only underground
and witnessed by only those who swear they too will utter cantos
in their turn, will gape and chirp like a Lazarus in a nest
of Purgatory, needing a bath and picnic wine poured into his visor.

8

Unthinkably suspended, face turned away while feet
could be facing us, perhaps vested in penitenza somehow
plumed and dangerous, perhaps inside-out and armored,
he sits on a bench and fritters his last day.
There is a landscape that only he sees somewhere
a place for us to meet him, somewhere an outraged jury
of his peers and all the evidence of things missing

in his life cannot howl in chorus, not even bothering
to wear the powdered wig or the Grecian mask, eyes
with that primal glance of cats who have sighted prey . . .
They have sighted nothing because he is missing
from their landscape, and he wills only to own himself
and to watch two streams converge in a single plane.

9

There is a place in the garden where I walk in circles
and contemplate the Y-Man, a patch of turned earth
of a transplanted tree, yielding to weight, the muddy roundedness
that was Y-Man's last legacy. I like to impress my step
slowly and with infinite eroticism make those glyphs and tropes,
touch imparting innocence, hearing him literally command
this particular route around this tree. Other voices are heard
harping from the exposed nature of earth, the shadowy, wormy
voices that are somehow the one voice of Baubo, commanding sweet
indignities; her pitiless undulations induce the perfection of trauma.
Trauma stands revealed as the god of Y-Man, the voice
that led him inexorably back to Baubo's relative generosity.
1 am only the transplanter of trees here.

10

I am only the one ordained not to be ordained . . .
He has the blessing of Baubo, no sky-gods admitted there.
"Mother Night" she is called by her friends; she is autoerotic
and ambidextrous and I suspect double jointed.
She is Y-Man's best fantasy of his cruel voyeur's eye
with license to explore every secret of her and your domination.
I have concluded that her encounter in such intimacy
prepared the contestants for their quick and repeated triggers
that claim solution where insoluble is the first barrier presented,
earthworks no problem with a backhoe parked in the driveway.
She is somewhere driven to exhibit herself, dreaming
of cloning herself "terra incognita," the inevitable avalanche
smothering all responses but those of eager oblivion.

11

The reason my cat follows me like a dog
is she likes my style . . . she likes the way I step
onto landings and seem to have a reason to pass through doorways.
She seems to understand, to even trust
my caged pacing or my obsessive grooming . . . and I get
this warm feeling that she is watching me
for tips on how best to be a cat.

1 call her Gretchen, my acrobat, my chaste bloom,
my statuesque perch in the twilight . . .
She has the gift of selective memory, and in this
it is I who am watching her for tips on being human,
I who fails to digest the unspeakable and leaves
the tortured trophy at the steps of the nearest temple . . .

12

The reason she has shown me this garden,
bone of my bone, is to see for myself in this mist
of rain and afternoon light the vivid glistening
of each leaf and petal and punctuating rocks.
There, a clump of furry buds with droplets,
everywhere, droplets cling to the tentacle horns
of various stages of columbine blossoming,
and she most at home thrilled by the cunning of accidental glory.
Inside, "psychoanalytic drawings" of Y-Man
are the featured display. His doodles reveal unnatural
anguish and crude satisfaction in separate species
locked in perverse embrace, fussy with mythology,
carving signs of passage on his nearest natural medium . . .

13

We can see the original manuscript of Trauma's adaptation

of *The Marriage of Y-Man*, first written by Y-Man's clocksmith

who married well and secretly supported republican rebels.

This comedy of manners has fully staged a lady's boudoir

where rivals and cuckolds hide in closets or under beds and witness

their worst nightmare celebrated with enthusiastic abandon.

Her soprano is the mewing of Gretchen, her gasps and alto groans

are as shameless as Baubo. We realized that on that day

of liberty and fraternity, when serpents refused to be trod upon,

when just beginning to fight was added to the motto "Plus Ultra,"

Y-Man discovered his mechanical hand extending from his armor.

From that day, his marriage was to the miracles of science

and their spawn of endless appetite for all things sensual.

14

Then she showed me her athletic body, right there

in the Roman antiquities section, opened her blouse

and peeled off her tights and like a backward uroboros,

the petals inside her furry pod exposed, took hold

of her own ankles and spoke my name from between suspended

billows of cumulus and rib cage arch, nipples just touching

the cold tile mosaic depicting a senator lifting his cup.

I caught the scent of old books, that musky blend of dust
and mold on aging paper. My father's copy of Balzac's *Ribald Tales*
with aquatints illustrating illicit courtly dalliance,
which I cherished in my pubescence unknown to parents,
is somewhere in this museum. I will content myself to admire
the back of her neck as she leans for a closer look at history.

15

The Divine Korey was conceived in Y-Man's mind of just such
a moment . . . It began with some notion of his rib as a faculty,
a kind of short-wave, more holy than our faculty of reason,
back when regions of the body could ring like the bells of treble
and peace in things uncertain was the milk of mother.
This faculty inside his chest, enshrined in votive frames depicts
immaculate hearts bleeding from a million wounds, the Divine One
moving to the podium where fate stares back from the sacred page.
Conceived in Y-Man's mind, the world gives birth to its destiny
beginning here with this child, blue-faced and staring at the light.
These are the Eleusian mysteries that suffuse the hidden years.
This is the intuition of "first principles," the square entering
the circle to form a mandala that is the "substance primordial . . ."

16

The contestants are having trouble with this category.

Their expressions are a chorus of unciform frowns,

eyes at the apogee of socket orbit, doom spelling itself

silently as references to the egg-born Eros sink in,

Hesiod's *Theogony* never included in their syllabus,

ontogeny considered bed time stories by Brothers Grimm

and useless for the coupling and uncoupling of hardware.

They can only wait for the return to a factual hierarchy,

endure this parabola of curved flight into far quadrants,

this picking of flowers while the underworld stalks unseen

and subsequent adventures of Divine Korey and her mother

on the journey to find the solar eyewitness to the rape.

They were the first contestants, their lunar lamp searching memory.

17

And anthropology, too, "as he met her once a-Maying,"

puzzles the contestants with the rites of Russian Wotyaks of Cura

when the harvest is threatened, how they carried their choice turf

in a wagon to the sacred grove of Cura, offering it

as bride, and the best of parties, to their restless god Keremet

This strategy was only half-successful, as probability would dictate.

They are at home now with the familiar rules of Pavlov

and the curve of statistics, that angelic chorus of contestants
tasting again their saliva and barking at the bell
for one more round of questions. These are they who will market
the consumption of information, knowledge on display
under glass like plastic facsimiles of lunch leftovers
by Claus or Andy, deconstruction the essence of structure . . .

18

. . . recognition the essence of what mystifies,
quotidian and omnipresent daytime dramas and prime time hype,
the agonies of constipation and its opposite answered
with authority at every commercial break.
The Divine Korey is not forgotten by Y-Man, even here.
I am only the installer of large household appliances,
screw driver in one hand, duck tape in the other,
instruction manual in my teeth. But the child that father's man
is emerging from every crack and cranny, Tintern Abbey
where vows are noble . . . from the garden, the somnambulance
of man is lit from within like a globe electrified, and Korey
stands in the garden with this globe glowing overhead,
owning her psychosis right into that rumored resurrection.

19

They have probably guessed she served as queen of Hades
and came in the dreams of even dying Aztecs to lead them
into that valley. Y-Man reminds me that Divine Korey
is a child, her gender essentially androgynous . . .
this is clear also from his drawings, called The Codex,
ideograms, the fermentation of the maguey plant for pulque
diagramed in detail, the maguey spines used for the jabbing
of misbehaving Aztec children. He learned early to bow to fate.
Here we see the moment of slavery, the victor reciting
"He is my beloved son," and the vanquished responding
to formula, "He is my beloved father." Eventual heart surgery
on the stone slab of Aztec epiphany was his destiny,
when eyes averted the contestants launched the Y-Man's arm.

20

It is now deployed as the Quibble Telescope, programmed
to photograph Orion Nebula, resulting in previously unseen
wisps and filaments from a newborn star, taking galactic
measurements, on alert for that rare asteroid
that some say wiped out the Titans who once ruled here.
These are candid snapshots of the gods, immutably fixing
each Olympian relationship as the spectrum of origins.

The universe knows the melody, she says, and the hymn
to Hermes is played for the contestants, the recording
at Mount Kyllene where Homer took furious notes
and they danced around a gigantic phallus of wood . . .
The words revolve around the themes of love and thievery . . .
She takes the ancient tortoise and constructs the lyre . . .

21

According to The Codex, Y-Man was like CIA or KGB.
He had the moral authority expected from professional guardians,
and it was used to eavesdrop on anything remotely suspicious.
He came home each night tired of always peeping and tailing,
his armor would clank up the stairs, and then elbow on knee
by the coffee table, Y-Man prophesied to the Divine Korey.
She would listen, holding the ionized globe in her lap,
and the patter of warnings gave way to the looking into continents.
Just so do our children challenge us to think how if its memory
we would have them trust, the eyes and not the ears
are what the mind feeds on like pups to patient udders,
and our voices are but signals in the wider hunt
for that buffalo we will strip clean for coming winter.

22

He asked her to picture this scene. You are stopped
at a light in Milford before turning to cross the bridge.
The flag is waving over the post office, a smiling
uniformed grandpa stands at the far corner and two girls
little older than Korey herself but filling tight cutoffs
with a promise on which life itself depends strolling
to your left, and you notice the proud chiming of the church,
its tower rising there in red brick. They both have Botticelli
ringlets, faces in distinct variations of that perfect loveliness;
they cross to greet grandpa like an animated Rockwell.
At their age the razzing, the picking of arguments is a style,
a fine art honed by genetic aggression and all those years
not yet lived that bitterly teach the necessity of compromise.

23

The bells go on chiming some hymn you can almost recognize.
The piety of Calvin and Luther is so cheerful.
The sovereignty of God never compromised even by free will.
No human act or intention can have merit before this God.
It must have been a liberation to so thoroughly abstract divinity
as to give it intimate commerce with all things secular.
State religion was convenient for both burghers and kings.

It must have widened the possibilities of drama, good humor
somehow infused into rigid taboos, civilized and ever so personal
that the Bard could stumble over it and weep . . .
Girls like these, already so audacious, are even free here
to rediscover things forbidden, tilings Gothic,
in the eyes and in the very throat of Y-Man . . .

24

And the ants are crawling all over him.
Insects love him because he is ample habitat,
young aspiring biologists would welcome the culture it would yield.
Have you considered how ants must have a perfect gyro,
as at home upside-down as right-side-up,
but at some decisive moment, at the very end of labyrinth
that could lead to the top of a tree, it gives up
and retracts all six tentacles at once,
dropping from all ground onto Y-Man here . . .
You admire this monument, see if you can shake loose
and feel the presence of his now only whispered complaints,
now a plaintive elegy accompanied by Korey across the air waves
authentically reproducing what was thought lost.

25

And I could tell her something about the losing of faculties
for that one voice that unconsumed is burning still
and all the baggage of exile, his life predicting history
and his work predicting his life, rendered almost immobile
by disappointed love, and then off a-courting,
consumed by something so Pre-Raphaelite that he never sees
it coming, this, my dropping cliché into our first toast . . .
I could at all cost avoid boring her,
as I shake loose those faculties nearly dormant
complete with the ghosts-of-the-flesh St Paul so shrewdly
described, a print as vivid as any sacrament claims . . .
that faculty on pins and needles, I am still prepared to defend
each and every disastrous decision one by one.

26

That she thinks I don't know what it is about me
is the first proof of true innocence. She demanded the definition
of its opposite, and all I could think to say was "death,"
considering it is that impression of eternity we relish
in abandonment to Eros that appears to us like innocence,
living innocence, walking upright and garlands in her hair,
who knows the best wines and is always free

to ransack my most private thoughts, always for sale
at the going price and she asks why a tattoo of a rat on my arm.
She is the first proof of how eternity is as innocent
as those bees that fertilize unknown to their stated purpose,
thinking only of honey, a queendom of honey well deserved
just for being the mortal enemy of death.

27

The inscription on this statue, with Y-Man leaning
elbow to knee, in full armor and strangely resembling
the American eagle, has edited out his crank, leaving the honey.
What commemorates this head across the shoulder
and this arms across beloved ourselves is gasping
exactly as those who feel star-crossed gasp in wonder,
the sadness already captured in the last wave.
I hope they were bishops, those who finally edited him.
He had it coming, with his theory of the solar system
and that arrogant way he thought he was the new Prometheus,
mocking even the Pope, he did, claiming he needed no white smoke
to take his place where keys unlock eternity,
declaring that all who disagree are baboons.

28

Seven in one qualifies as a world book record

in the grand profession of giant-killing . . .

I am only the sniffer of flowers here . . .

1 am only the receiver of bills here, of calls

to renew warranties, of uncomprehending response to each

appeal for what the blues has earned a citizen and taxpayer.

My tentacles to this world are of my own fashion.

I learned this from Y-Man. He called it adaptation to circumstance,

or improvisation, or that up-beat in the down

that keeps even the contestants honest in their off-time,

trading tips on how to beat the merciless machine of chance

with all their voodoo mixed in with their science,

their salt tossed freely over their left shoulders.

PART TWO

29

They say the gods become jealous when a man claims
seven in one. When it took the gods seven days to make a world
and someone like me has made seven worlds in one day
it upsets the balance, and punishment soon follows.
The first sign was how the questions to the contestants
kept returning to Y-Man and his more elusive Korey,
and their dumbfounded agonies of silence, their pitiful
heads shaking in ignorance was like watching the Christians turn
and eat the lions, and the nation tuned-in to witness
this carnage so clinically calculated for ratings.
A question was asked, "Who was called biggest boy,
and whose sanctuary was a cave in Mt. Dikte,"
and I rose and shouted, "It is Y-Man!"

30

"Like Mohammed," I continued, "when he left the cave,
still beardless and the sun and moon both shining,
he made giant footprints, although a man like you or me."
These contestants were driving all programming to a test pattern
with their silence, and silence was never a friend to Y-Man.
They relied on his Quibble telescope, his arm still orbiting
and gathering data, but knew nothing of the hero behind it.

They could quote from his monument and date *The Codex*,
and tell the stories of how the scrolls were discovered
that proved he had existed, that he was founder of our introspection
and founder of our machines by his analogic multiplications
and metaphoric hyperboles, but the contestants
were oblivious to his story or his voice . . .

31

I had thrust myself into the game, which no longer was a game
as the contestants voted to change the format
to resemble *20/20* or *60 Minutes* to investigate Y-Man,
Contestant #1: "Do you claim to have deciphered *The Codex*?"
"I do," I said, "but only because the faulty mirror in Quibble
allows its lens to be trained on the text here below
so I can read it like a genome series, every letter and trope
in the DNA legible be it junk or current masterpiece..."
The ordinarily pleasant moderator tore his blazer up the back
and abruptly resigned. I was shown to the witness stand.
Contestant #2: "Are you saying that Y-Man is alive?"
"I am saying that I hear his voice, that the radio beam
relayed to earth from Quibble follows me everywhere."

32

Contestant #3: "Can you ask the Quibble questions and relay
the answers of Y-Man?" I thought of Gretchen faithfully
waiting at home for the fishy plate she loves, and strange
association, how Y-Man calls for the daily sacrifice of fish.
He says it was because in the hidden years in the town
from which nothing good was expected, he had a backyard spring
that formed a pond with multicolored fishes always undulating.
"I can relay his answers if I close my eyes."
Why not let them probe? They feel like orphans knocking
on his vault, as I too felt before his voice became distinct,
and it was rather like the barbershop trance
to let him speak to the millions as he had spoken to me,
to let them trim my hackles with their young, fashionable hands.

33

For me it began with the Divine Korey, he said,
with the class play in which she had the central role
of Turnip in *The Big Turnip*. The play opens with Grandmother
trying to pull the giant turnip out of the ground, and failing,
Grandfather pulls on Grandmother, then the boy on Grandfather,
then the dog pulls the boy, then the cat, and finally the bird
biting the cat's tail is critical mass for Korey to pop forth.

I opened my eyes and explained that Y-Man speaks in riddles,

especially in the spotlight, and his fuse could get short,

but that *The Codex* will read like a FAX machine to mankind

only if the story of Divine Korey is heard,

only if the riddle of her being is cracked.

At this point I announced a station break for our sponsor.

34

Contestant #4: "Please, before we hear about Korey, tell us

of Y-Man's origins and life . . ." I closed my eyes, and Y-Man spoke:

My name in the beginning was "He Who Looks at the World."

My mother was Baubo, cast from heaven and falling

to the banks of the River Ob, two ribs from under

her right armpit broke out. I was born with golden hands and feet.

Therefore, I called my father Trauma of Heaven.

I was taught, as *The Codex* describes, through beatings

and once was left for dead on a dunghill by my uncle

who had clubbed me unmercifully with a mammoth bone.

It was there that I first heard Trauma, my real father,

and he taught me how to use my golden hands and feet.

35

I became horseback, some called me Strong Hans,
and my epiphanies of vengeance on my tormentors is legendary.
My prowess was partially due to my diet, which Baubo
provided first from the milk of wolves and then
from the meat of the ocean's primeval tortoise.
I forged a dynasty on the good counsel of Trauma
and built roads and founded many charitable institutions,
but always with a predator's eye for that magic dance.
I founded the "Dance of Golden Hands and Feet Alliance"
and supported the arts, helped raise money for the stage,
and on that stage performed my most savage consummation:
I gave birth to my Divine Korey, or she to me
remains the question I would ask of you . . .

36

"He Who Looks at the World" wore impenetrable armor
on stage, loneliness peculiar to things primordial
he was decked in the scales of mother deep, but gleaming
with reflection on precise joints and functional plates
all molded to the body in the finest metaphors available.
His Korey makes her first appearance picking flowers on the bank
of the River Ob, which flows into the lower realm

known today as Tartarus, and "He Who Looks at the World"
sees her kill a tortoise and from it fashion a lyre.
He vows to make her his bride, but learns how on that day
an unseen beetle had bitten that child and a deadly microbe
migrated in her blood with neurological damage in mind.
From that day forward he called himself Y-Man.

37

I cannot speak for the contestants, but I
reacted to his story with a certain incredulity.
I have a neighbor whose wife became obsessed with
the exact Latin transcription of "Little Purple Rubber Duckie,"
(the Latin for "rubber" being a particular challenge)
and the next day her husband actually saw a purple duck
while gazing from the Frenchtown Bridge, went to tell everyone,
and no one believed him. But I have seen demonstrated
a floating rock; my nephew Luke found it in the stream,
a microbe's labyrinthine paradise by Medusa,
capillaries of air that volcanic heat had pumped into matter
and we now call igneous tufa. At least he never claimed
that Korey rose bodily from this planet and disappeared.

38

"May I ask Y-Man why the letter 'Y*' in his name?"
asked contestant #1. I opened my eyes
and could see from the furious activity of technicians on the set
that we were still live, and most likely were now carried
on all major networks, including CNN, with programs bumped
like this was the Gulf War or Kennedy's assassination, teenagers
across the country no doubt stamping their feet in frustration.
"He will not answer that question. He will maybe joke
like Police about the YMCA, or he will allude
to the famous chromosome, or the shape of the letter
being like a divining rod for hidden springs . . ."
It was long past due for a commercial; bladders
from coast to coast were relieved when it came.

39

Next they showed a film clip of those who discovered
The Codex, second only in history to when King Josiah
decided to renovate the Jerusalem Temple and unearthed
the original Pentateuch right there on the precincts.
Y-Man had retired to his cave following "the rape."
He vowed to create microscopic enemies to the virus
that attacked his Korey. He imagined legions of synthetic artifice,

like Athenians in manly love and loyalty, one wall
of overwhelming force against that Baubo-sent virus.
He started with the theory of dragon's teeth planted.
But it was Ezekial's worst nightmare . . .
He progressed from here to an understanding of time depth
and a proto-language and superstring theory of quarks . . .

40

I was prepared to discuss the Y-Man's methodology,
but contestant #2 was clearly eager to cut to the chase:
"What happened to Divine Korey when she knew she was doomed?"
At last they wanted to know about her, and Y-Man spoke
although my eyes were open, like in the times of Baubo:
"She became mad. She insisted a witness to her rape,
if only the sun, would cure her with his testimony.
I saw nothing that day but the River Ob
and Korey forging music from my mother's nursery.
I remember thinking how my amazing arm was the perfect flute.
I was burned-out from management's demands
and when I heard that music we could make . . . but I digress.
She appears to me in dreams commanding my research.

41

She has told me how she followed the river to its mouth
and how the subatomic world has limits to infinite mass
and binding energy, that the infinite confining potential
proven mathematically to be limited is also limitless,
more like a machine than anyone would have guessed."
"Machine?" contestant #3 chimed in, "you say the underworld
is a machine?" Y-Man had seen many inquisitions, and misplaced
words were usually the seed of ruin, so he prompted me:
"The Divine Korey only meant that since photon wave functions
appear to collapse into definite particles when asked nicely . . ."
This seemed to pacify them, and Y-Man explained to me
that all is nominal to them; their dogma is that photon functioning
is collectively conferred and recommended to nonexistent heaven.

42

I wondered if Y-Man ever asked Korey about if Newton
really took a holiday in subatomic space, or worked
part-time under the table in the legendary Tartarus.
That she had seen reality in all its cruel monstrosity and still
eternity clings to her like a mother, under microscope
and under telescope both, they keep searching for the witness.
Contestant #4 held up a copy of *The Codex.*

"Y-Man, when you left your cave to redeem her,
why did you not be her witness then?"
"I was only El Presidente there," he said,
"not a god as you know me here. My witness
is *The Codex*, which heaven dictated in ninety days
and I imposed on my subjects regardless of persuasion."

43

Like the Lapplanders following the grazing instincts
of their wild herds of reindeer, we had always followed Y-Man
across wide fiords or to the very toenails of the Ice Age.
But what began as a documentary suddenly changed and became
like a Senate select committee hearing on alleged pubic hair.
Y-Man went from the top to the bottom of the polls
in 24 hours, and the hearings continued with all other programs
sent to re-run limbo in a milling corral of antlers.
It all came out, his dirty deal with microbes to trade their tyranny
for one glimpse of galaxy collision birthing new stars.
"You no longer heard my voice, so secret police were necessary
to tap phones and compile detailed dossiers on philistines
and revisionists prone for Baubo's seductions."

44

"Is it then the case," asked contestant #1, "that you

abandoned the Divine Korey to her fate?"

"No!" he screamed through my vocal chords.

"She is my egg with wings, my icon of persona robed in philosophy.

"Is it then true you invented her to bear the guilt

of your mother's murder by the River Ob?"

"My mother lives," he said, but he knew they meant her symbol

in the tortoise, its shell mounted and painted with sun-burst.

"And the curse was hers to carry, was Korey's, is that correct?"

The time had long passed to plead the Fifth Amendment.

"It is true I have profited, as have you all, by taming Baubo,

by snatching away, as Goethe did his mother's red fur coat

and skating in triumph around the rink to impress his friends . . ."

45

There is a play by Heinrich von Kleist in which

Achilles is killed by Penthesilea, the Amazon queen,

instead of the standard patriarchal version by Homer.

It is clear the two warriors are well matched,

neither able to dominate the field, but suddenly we know

Achilles wants to lose. Three times he throws away his sword.

He appears to be in a trance, and like a zombie turns his neck

for her arrow to pierce, falls, Penthesilea savagely rips away
his armor and, with her dogs, tears away his chest with her teeth . . .
This has something of what happened to Y-Man next.
He volunteered everything, how he bootlegged volumes by de Sade
from a large leather-bound suitcase on Avenue E last Tuesday,
everything . . . how the beetle in question was his agent . . .

46

They thrust *The Codex* before the lens of Quibble in my eyes
and opened to the part still undeciphered called
"psychoanalytic drawings," and sure enough
the Y-Man was revealed as a schizoaffective, convinced
he would someday create the primordial substance
like a block of cheese made by Carthusian monks.
His enemies were identified as "time" and "silence"
in this centuries-long struggle to elude entropy, Tartarus,
by cutting cheese to the next generation, 100% fat free.
All this was transparent compensation for unresolved control issues
expressed in sadomasochistic obsessions that resembled
all too vividly the scene of Y-Man's humiliation
on prime-time on all major networks, including CNN.

47

Everything changed after the indictment of Y-Man,
although on the surface things went back to normal.
I went home to my cat and the back-hoe in the driveway
and the contestants would now include the date of his trial
as a fact in their memory-banks. I never heard his voice again.
I sometimes wonder if somehow Baubo planted a poison beetle
on Y-Man too, with the virus that compels conquest finally
naked as the virus that compels being utterly conquered.
More than one alleged hero ended his days in a self-made bunker.
Or was it the cruel pedagogy of his father Trauma?
"We may never know," I can see myself saying to America
in that up-coming documentary:"He Who Looked at the World."
We also may never know what Divine Korey meant to him.

48

In the old days I would have these encounters with Korey
that I think now were holograms sent by Quibble,
but reflect I think the secret mind of Y-Man.
I usually saw her in the garden, chasing insects
or just standing with that eerie luminous globe
held over her head like a beach ball she refuses to throw.
She could sometimes seem older, a young woman

with great expectations, say a student biologist,
and she would drink in the colors and smells of my garden,
and I always felt so flattered, and then she would tell me
there was something about me that made her breathless,
so I gave her my breath as best I could
until she vanished just like always in the sound of crickets.

49

I would often see her down by the creek. Once I saw her
swimming, and she was singing something that repeated the word
"magnetosphere" with an Icelandic yodel in a minor key,
and I know Y-Man was trying to tell me something.
He always loved riddles, but with today's video technology
the possibilities of obscurity are endless.
Sometimes I think I see her in a woman I meet.
This happened not long ago on a date.
In the garden outside the museum she was child Korey,
and inside she was woman Korey, and we all know what happened
in the Roman antiquities section . . . I'm not sure
if this isn't just another perversion of Y-Man's mind
that he sends his Korey to haunt me on Pentecost Sunday.

50

I have always had occasion to ponder the kindergarten portraits
of now estranged paramours. In gilded frames, they found
their way to prominent display in each home, each eager face,
really the same face now that I mentally compare, black and white
and adorable in ruffled dress with chubby legs dangling.
The painful smile was probably the lights,
but I always thought I could see some terminal sadness there.
Maybe they knew these photos would have this effect, and is why
they always emerged from boxes when I arrived.
How could I have guessed that my own face
would acquire that look, the gazing into nothing present
like a "boy's own paper" Jungle Jim, mounting his howdah
and off through tall grass into nowhere found easily.

51

The contestants were right to discredit Y-Man.
Their received doctrine of the substantiality of human personality
was consistent with all his research, which had proved
that all consciousness is a construct of language
and not of any ground of being in the origins of life.
They merely reached his own conclusion when they closed *The Codex*
and extinguished his throwback mystifications and weird locutions.

There were sightings of Y-Man from time to time
that became a national joke, and the post office
took a poll as to whether his picture on a new stamp
should be with his visor up or down, which itself
was a joke as either way no one saw his eyes.
Dissertations on Y-Man's blind spot multiplied.

52

But there is one theory that carries his name
and remains the subject of intense scientific inquiry.
For him it was a throw-away idea, although at one time
he believed it would unlock the secret of that "winged egg"
that would somehow heal his Korey and explain the universe both.
He called it his Particle Theory, which proposed hypothetical fields
specifically designed to break the symmetry of forces and particles.
These Y-fields, uniform in strength across space and therefore
minimal in energy, would follow the same equations of motion
that govern electric and magnetic fields, but unlike them
Y-fields do not drop to zero in its lowest energy state.
Instead, it takes on a particular nonzero strength everywhere.
This breaks the symmetry of forces and particles there coupled.

53

Y-Man's particle theory would seem to explain both cosmic
and subatomic phenomena of symmetry-breaking.
It explains the very acquiring of mass. Just as ice consists
of crystalline planes having definite orientations,
so the Y-field can be pictured as taking on a certain direction,
much like Marco Polo with his compass needle in fact reading
how the earth's magnetic field is breaking the symmetry of space.
But in this case, the electroweak Y-field breaks the symmetry
of electron and neutrino "space." The direction
in which it points acquires mass and becomes the electron.
Hence, the topological defects observed in the galaxies is explained,
those intense bunchings of energy which retain the "infant universe"
cradled in clumps of matter by equivalence of energy and mass.

54

To test his theory, Y-Man became a cyclotron,
which he always claimed is why he seemed to vanish.
He really only extended his armor plating, added concrete,
and made his mind a huge empty tube in which to accelerate matter.
He spun it with his rapid alterations of polarity and threw atoms
like Pollock throws paint, searching the results for patterns.
This was the real meaning of his "psychoanalytic drawings"

that now are banned as sadomasochistic.
But like most good theories, the more evidence he gathered
the more theories were needed to account for what he saw.
The Divine Korey was not forgotten even here.
At night he would sleep in his concrete bunker looping twenty miles
and a woman would appear, her strings and his flute . . . equivalent.

55

The melody they made was in the nonzero strength of Y-field
and pointed a direction against the balance of their polarities.
It would seem to him their music was eternal, although he knew
it only led to particle clods and the occasional supernova.
In his dream he would look at her, and she was too much woman
to be Korey, too particular as person, too articulate
as nothing his enemy, time, could ever master...
and in that sleep the formula came clear that Plato tried to paint
in the cave of Socrates, and the woman was not Korey at all
but her mother, a maiden when she dragged him from the dunghill
and washed him clean, his whole body and not just those golden
hands and feet, and fed him at the risk of bee-sting
the nectar from the blossoms of her infinite care.

56

I awake unsure if it was my dream or his dream.

Only a madman would bury himself in concrete,

or a victim like Jimmy Hoffa, and I am after all

only the casual visitor to museums here, and the watcher

of contestants who can blaze through unrelated facts.

I am also Gretchen's reason for purring and my own reason

for saying "magnetosphere" out loud to the haze

that hangs along the creek and in the leaves above.

I am a portrait of leisure, backing off from tasting both power

and grace, impenitent keeper of time, and now of silence.

Korey and her mother were last seen along the Amazon River,

photographed here waving from their never-seen century

to our capsulized virtuality of all space.

PUZZLE ME BACK

PUZZLE ME BACK

Tonight I'm tempted to arrange my calendar
like some Noah with a dove up his sleeve,
to sober up in the face of your Hebrew acrostics
and stack myself like multiple video screens that
puzzle me back to you . . . My Gentile ways somehow
file past two by two: Le giraffe du Mute Longing,
Das Hippo von Infamous Immersions, that Trumpet King
already charging . . . In the trees, shrill supplication.
I'm tempted to be grateful this Rosh Hashanah,
this Feast of Angels, this heavenly Chapter Twelve.

FROTH FOR MELINDA

A man wants the froth to billow
when she makes herself generous.
He is pointed with his screen dynamics.
She is Mona Lisa with her naughty thoughts.

A man wants his missiles precision guided
and perfect in their score, the target owned,
the flush straight. She pours her cubes into shots
and dashes all hope with her coiled heel.

She too knows how to point,
but it is past his shoulder to another more amusing froth.
He turns his head as she laughs, as the juke box
clunks into the groove that wins us both.

SANGRIA AND GUITAR STRINGS

(for Carol G.)

A match made in heaven hovers.
Unscrewing the Sangria bottlecap.
Twisting guitar pegs. Same same.

Wrist and fingers, opposing thumb.
Only counterclockwise pressure.
Unsealed spirits, wound taut the strings.

Strings the taut wound, spirits unsealed.
Pressure counterclockwise only.
Thumb opposing, fingers and wrist.

Same same. Pegs guitar twisting.
Bottlecap Sangria the unscrewing.
Hovers heaven in made match A.

EMPTY SPACE

Does nothing turn out to be something?
In mathematics, sure. But in physics?
Einstein's formerly disgraced theory rears:
The cosmic constant, known today as
dark matter, is empty space proven a
Thing (of a different stripe) with a gravitylike
force that contradicts actual gravity and propels
each galaxy at an accelerating rate away
from each other until empty space reigns.

The void of space is like a springing coil
hurling all true and marvelous thingness away.
The void in souls is the dark matter loneliness
growing ever-faster such that now it takes
one person with whom to discuss politics,
another religion . . . This one satisfies just comedy.
Next I'll need a different person for each shade
of each passion I need . . . And so forth, until
the absence of someone to talk to reigns.

A NEW SHERIFF IN TOWN

Let's say your boss tells you that the HCSIS ("hicks us") report
that you thought you had to write is assigned to someone else.
The world can suddenly open up in a moment like that.
Befriending time, even, seems credible.
Great deeds suddenly loom on the horizon. Even the Hydra
of your ugly desk litter, usually snorting insolently all around you,
now blanches when it sees your face.
It sees the face of one liberated from writing a HCSIS report,
a face that all random and pregnant procrastination should fear.
Word gets out fast that there's a new sheriff in town.
Now the desperately screaming need for filing pleads and spits
in their limbo on your desk. They know that you're going in.

MAD COW

We have been waiting for you since forever.
You've dabbled too long with the king's esthetes.
(There should be a law against a limp wrist
without due sexual persuasion to explain it!)

You even mounted Canada's Mounties before me!
I'm sure you have a good reason. "Disease"
is better than most. Mouth frothing gets my attention.
Radiation treatment puts me prone before statues.

There is nothing about lighting candles per se that
interests me. I am smart enough to fear sculpture.
But when they said they split the cow's hemisphere
across its spinal column, my rectum fluttered like a leaf.

RIHAB TAHA (Dr. Germ)

She may be no bathing beauty, but she has that virus
that brings presidents and Mao-faced gangsters to their knees.
She has that knowing look that makes men crazy, over the shoulder

looking at you like she can see your need to refinance your mortgage,
like she can snap her finger, and faster than 7-7-2, this Rajheed
better spring Aphrodite-like from his lab, test-tubes in both hands.

He had better have the incriminating evidence well hidden.
He had better guard that virus with his life.
What virus? Show me what you think you know about murder.
I'm so innocent, the driven snow looks filthy by comparison.
Plunge your lens into my bloodstream! You'll find nothing.

She may be no seaside promenade, but she has detonation.
She packs her own cosmic parachute and fail-safe visor.
She kisses worldwide germs hello, then good-bye and God speed.

CAT SCAN
(To the goddesses Hathor and Bastet on Valentine's Day, 2004)

Well ain't that the unrolling of a mummy!
CAT scan radiation reveals a cross-section of
Ramses' skull. Here, the scars of sucking out
his brains through his sinuses. Most organs must be
removed and mummified soon after death and kept
in canopic jars. The brains are liquefied and flushed.
The point is to advertise to the spirit-world: "Me."
The point is seduction of gods . . . of being a still target
for the howling birds above to swoop and claim me.
How those embalmers would admire our endoscopy.
How I admire their most ancient science: *Oh my heart,*
you who stands up with me like a mother, desert me not
on the day of judgment inscribed on a jade scarab
placed sincerely over the place where my heart once was.

REMBRANDT

What a stink over "The Night Watch," with all those
important personages treated like grand cabbages!
The scandal toppled poor Rembrandt, here Charles Laughton,
from his tipsy success in polite Flemish society.
It finally drove him out of Amsterdam
and back to his peasant roots, the village
from which he escaped twenty years before
to revel in the civilized abandon to notions.
His uncle greets him in the way of peasants,
clutches his hand as if apparitions are daily pleasures.
The meal is only just ready, and as guest
he opens The Book over steaming yams and potatoes
and reads the bitter story he would rather hide.
He weeps. We have already seen the greater loss,
his beloved Saskia, proclaimed by him by invitation
in a tavern as his inspiration, no, his life . . . now gone.
He attempts a certain rutting in the sawdust there.
But rather than seeking therapy, he returns
to Amsterdam still convinced he is a painter.
What happens next is a whirlwind of fate.
The serving girl, newly hired in his house,
is exactly the model he needs for his next painting.

She is a country girl, Elsa Lanchester, known best
as Frankenstein's bride, but in Rembrandt's life
she is Enrika. She takes to modeling like a champ.
She isn't put off by his roughness because all she sees
is the gentility he brings to each and every moment,
how much he really loves the light and what it does.
She begins to love his light wherever it takes her,
and she ultimately becomes his agent against creditors,
saving his paintings from the ignominy of state property.
But poor Rembrandt is destined to lose his Enrika,
taken in mid-remodeling of The First Seduction.
We last see him entertaining young people in a tavern
with his wit and haunting references, an old man
alone and daily desperate for funds
who forgoes food for another trip for art supplies.
We see him booted out of the tavern
smelling of fish, and back to the studio
to finish his self-portrait. "All is vanity," he says
to himself in the positioned mirror, his last words
to his young friends in the tavern. As if Hollywood
would have us believe that art is a hopeless task
best left to professionals like themselves. But I swear,
he winked in that positioned mirror.

THERE IS A HOUSE

There is a house, doomed on a pie-shaped tot, windswept
And humble here, colonial farmhouse among the postmodern.
Perched on the Mountain of Beauty, paint peeling, sorry for
So much excess of interior weather, it boasts of no termites.

Choirs of perennial songhood live on inside its cracks, keeping
Yet the Logos denied elsewhere, sailing yet from Caffa while
Mongols catapult plague-ridden bodies into history's fortress,
Refusing forever to dock where saboteurs shake hands.

This house has examined the war in its bowels and was not
Struck dumb. It burned its lights from dormered windows late
Into each night of each season, and has issued mixed reports
In the chimney smoke that once rose from its unspeakable roof.

RE-MUSAL

A single challenge makes its Holy Ghost descent.
As in Gospel times, this is a public event. But rather than
taking place along the Jordan it takes place in Fishtown.
It's a birthday party. The honored guest is only one year old.

The challenge is a proposal of marriage. For such as these
who face each other this night there is nothing but themselves.
No theme of social continuity, no classic romance, no history.
There is only free will suddenly rearing its head above loss.

And what is it that was lost? No one really knows. It goes by
many names: True Sight, Action Known, Habit Dead, Love Felt.
We all silently agree to not mention the loss for the child's sake.
She will learn of it soon enough. But this proposal owes nothing

to the hope for children or even childhood's renewal. It is, simply,
the birth of True Sight, Action Known, Habit Dead, Love Felt.
It is adulthood alone, for one instant, freed from Sigmund's traumas
and Charlie's pointing monkeys, it is re-musal in one breath.

PLAUSIBLE STRUCTURES

Now he can hunt the crocodile fearlessly. Scarred
and scaly, it's that crisis of surgery again, and welcome.
It is a coiled spring that floats beneath the surface.
The logic of body-piercing dawns: It is the "Cavatti,"
the mile-long Tai Pusan parade in Singapore,
the pierced initiates walking inside forty pounds
of aluminum rods each. It is the Warholian exhibitionism.
Let's face it; it's the packaging. But it's also human skin.
I can imagine how he felt, parading as that living contradiction,
the boxing himself into himself his statement of plausible
structures, expansion redefined as points along the vast
uncharted ocean of the skin become land, become grid
locating the unseen scars within the tissue of it,
the earth that may yet prove indigestible to entropy.

O CRUX AVE

No artful dodging on the avenue of crux
but dodging of a positivistic stripe
at least, with a gift for some daffy ducks.

If this man of thorns could actually type
the sign they've hung above his head,
he'd word it in the second person and wipe

that smile off my face. He is not dead.
He is fleeting, yes, since I cannot read.
My eyes are fists. No, they are lead.

Scourge tips to the man of great need.
Illiterate one, you who won't dodge,
decipher this. He is not freed.

Look away, Dixieland. Build your lodge
on the crux of only the soft, the warm,
the looking, not the getting out of Dodge.

ADAM'S REFUGE

It is said there is a cave where Adam took refuge after the fall.
He found solace there in an angel's melancholy lullaby of future
rocky paths and awesome voyages. She has been this cave to me.
She taught me that angel's song long before my first reluctant breath.
She was all there is of home for me. I was first among her brood
of restless offspring, our images covering the walls of that refuge,
one of many bending ears for the harmony she longed to share.
I was first to gaze with her on Redemption's vast landscape.
She is now part of that landscape, released from Adam's cave.
And I am released from the cave she was to me, adrift in sky.

I FIRED THE OPTOMETRIST

If reduced to being priest of a cargo cult, at least
be it known that I fired the optometrist.
If suddenly utopian, or new age interlopian,
be it known that I fired the optometrist.
If I'm found like Edison, bulbous, opening worm cans,

all ocular occult and trembling diphthong,
or found stringing No Mind in the Nothing Much, you'll find
at least I fired the optometrist, and so, at least
I fired that Rasputin ugly face of his.
At least my cornea is still mine.

The time may come when I will have to poison him.
I have anthrax stored in despotic depot palaces.
Do not think from this that I am a schismatic heretic,
just because the ocean beds are not my problem.
My problem is not empiricism, not mysticism, not even positivism,

my problem is ending senile depending on him.
Empire takes a new mask , not so much the look
of legions building Hadrian's Wall as unseen hands
that reach up our puppet skirts and diddle freely.

The Blue Heron

Empire has no political wing exclusively sighted
near or far. It knows how the brain makes its own
hegemony by predictable laws. Empire needs no face
to smile and squint, compare and contrast, to rule
itself the only game in town, stretching fools
on the rack of what is true by what is best.

FALLING IN LOVE

Falling in love should be normative.
It should be the surgeon's joy in handling the
instruments of incision, rapturously engrossed in
the palpable distinction between disease and
normative miraculous organic design.
It should be mind wrapping around other mind
in a mutual cocoon from which both emerge new.

It should be something more than taking notes
while waiting for the laundry's next cycle or
discovering New Jersey in a broken kitchen tile.
What's normative should not be counting on
discovery of The Union beneath my tile work or
dreading the cost of a Louisiana Purchase.
It should be finding the lost penny and celebrating.

IN THE CHOIR OF ST. LAZARUS

. . . upon release I wax epistemological, your innocence
when I with antiphon in hand approach you, behold
thrashing in the ashes, no leper as foretold . . .

foretold without warmth or flex, not as I and you
can play, unbowed by polyphony, alas, it is my true
amazement that we can nail firmly flight's immanence,

erecting me by contrast over yet another tympanum, he
who made me inscribed where I froze, it burns
with ambition regardless . . . mine on contradictions turns,

a Becket cathedral-bound or disembodied voices said
in prosody's arch liberties, words themselves are dead
on arrival, come near with soprano keenness and see . . .

WAVING AND HEAVING

Poiein anaphoran (poetic up-carry)

TO CONNIE ON A COLD NIGHT IN MARCH (Matins)

Don't let the crackle of new heat
        in these old pipes fool you.
These radiators have blazed all winter.
        Empty they have not been
for as far back as memory now reaches.
        The windows, I admit, leak
frozen drafts I fear that seep ectoplasmic
        alien abductors.
One of them once tiptoed into my bedroom,
        but it only slipped between the sheets
and spooned me in the dark. I saw no insect face,
        sensed no evil will
to probe and dissect another infidel.
        I tried to move. It vanished.
But I digress. Don't be fooled by all this random
        slush and clatter. Actually
my building intones a monk's neum and punctum,
        a solfeggio guided by
the Guidonian hand of an Ossian poet.
        I must prepare the text,
something like: "The drafts of March
        hath pierce-ed to the rrroot."

Tad Cornell

FELONIOUS PHYLOGENY (Lauds)

At the Tango, the "Cambrian explosion" is manifest.
> There is no common ancestor
that explains the simultaneous burst, the biological
> big bang of sudden variety
from species through genus all the way to kingdom
> that comes of the fossil evidence!
Darwin is on the ropes!
> At the Tango all such irreverence
for that Warholian high priest is celebrated.
> The guests at the Tango
raise their beakers and cheer
> for a son's success in music, say,
or the death of notions that justify villainy,
> or the sad day Baghdad Bob bid us adieu.
Darwin struggles from his costume before our eyes.
> For him the Tango is Guantanamo Bay.
This pathetic terrorist is exposed here,
> his one-horse theory proving unworthy
of his suicidal melodramas.
> You saw yourself caging him
like a catechumen at the altar rail.

You proposed, on his part, a change of heart.

    Fat chance!

He has long since taken the Pons Assenorum! (Bridge of Asses)

    He will be the ass, history's figure of fun.

Witness his idiotic ranting on how filibustering

    would have stopped the rise of Hitler.

Watch him hold his donkey ears and chant "*La, la, la* . . .

    I can't hear you, I can't hear you, *la, la, la* . . ."

NO TORTURE HERE (Prime)

You saw yourself caging him like a catechumen at the altar rail.

You were clear on how this oblique awakening

remains oblique between the magnetic poles of past and future.

Quality of life is no absolute category.

Darwin was thrashing in his cage.

By his logic we should pull his plug.

He prays five times daily to his social engineering Mecca.

He goes on with his cliché manifestos of nature's brutal contest.

He goes on shaping an Abstract Man from his mud.

His interrogations had become your central duty in life.

Sometimes you have played it "good cop/ bad cop."

Reverse psychology can have him stammering in mid rationalization.

The virgins in his paradise would be raped by his phylum sort.

At the Tango, fellow interrogators meet to compare notes.

This is quality of life.

This is where past lessons and world destiny walk among us

like Jehovah walked with Adam and Eve.

They manifest to us as St. Patrick and St. Joseph,

a feast in the midst of Lent.

Quality is living gratitude for snakes dispatched
and family cradled, for Scythian dances danced and
Rilke poems declaimed . . .
The fraud of colon cleansing is scorned at the Tango.
The only torture here is self-imposed.
Meanwhile, the supposed vegetative Terri cries out "I WANT . . ."
to the consternation of Darwin's medical goons.

IRREDUCIBLE ACTION (Terce)

At the Tango, fellow interrogators meet to compare notes.
Theirs is a celebration of their daily giving what is due
to this Cambrian explosion of conjugal life.
We cannot help but kneel in awe of the irreducible action behind it.
Papers are presented proving the existence of the moral natural law
in scientific terms, confounding Darwin's claim
that it is extinct. Could his genocidal jihad against it
have had something to do with the killing field that
he and his goons present us?
(There was general acclamation.)
Could he have murdered the last notion of "ought"
to wear the dignified vestments of reason that will proceed from
a homo sapien? No!
(We raised our beakers and cheered.)
Symposiums are given on the latest techniques for caging those
Darwin yetis that feed so freely on our children
like the tiger circling a Napal village.
Anthems are sung extolling the cognition of what should be the true
pope of everything rational. Hymns are sung to the action
that is person. The bread of life is actually consumed.

Tango is no figment, you who whine and curse in your cage.

Be not afraid. We will not pull out your feeding tube.

You are a treasure of information.

You too serve virtue, however unwittingly.

If anyone among us fails in this, may he join Darwin.

But be certain of one thing.

Monistic abstraction in black robes

ought not continue tyranny over the Constitution.

IMAGINE UNION (Sext)

Papers are presented proving the existence of the moral natural law.

But it was she who could see the unseen that presented best.

Results should be the crown of choice, she said,

not handcuffed to itself and made to beg.

Her freedom is circumscribed like the ovary-shaped colonnades

by aerial view of St. Peter's.

She honors the tiniest intention to choose wisely.

She never leaves her own abandoned, and her own is all.

For her, these precipitous times are business as usual.

Her constancy looms like an apparition over the Tango.

Looking up, I see the tower of her house and marvel.

I saw the family portraits on the vast walls and marveled.

I marvel all along the winding Lincoln Drive that

past engineers had cut through craggy Pennsylvania hills.

My ceilings are tall, but hers are simply monumental.

Her sufferings too are monumental.

Polyglot motets go from Romanesque to Gothic on the car stereo.

My tower is coming up.

Papers were presented proving the existence of the moral natural law.

But it was she who could imagine union who made union.

My building intones a monk's neum and punctum,
a solfeggio guided by the Guidonian hand of an Ossian poet.
I must continue the text,
something like: "Sewn in dishonor but raised in glory,
oh death, you have no sting."

DON'T TAKE IT PERSONALLY (None)

The fraud of colon cleansing is scorned at the Tango.
We value too late the "good bacteria" in and outside
our bowels, critters we rely on to survive at all. We, the victims
of antibacterial soap and Darwin's fetish for colon cleansing,
salute you. Don't take it personally. Darwin is a siren in the mosque.
He can flap his big eyelashes through an iconoclast's grid
and have you marching against yourself to obliterate all microbes.
He can make the virtue of cleanliness into a high crime.
He would pick anyone with whom to share his mission, anyone
who gets the romance of mass depersonalization: Utopia.
Dateline: Human dandruff threatens the stratosphere.
Swirling clouds block the sunlight, hasten global warming
(or global cooling), and drop untold disease
on unsuspecting Third World villages.
Who knew my psoriasis would be a weapon of mass destruction?
We should come clean with Darwin on our lethal head scratching.
What nightmares he'd suffer knowing our Tango think tanks
produce cyclones of dandruff that sail the trade winds, migrating like
birds conferring in mid air before diving into his soup.
The fraud of perfect privacy is also scorned at the Tango.

"Every man an island" was Luther's biggest blunder.

But it was Darwin and his central committee lobbing heads Jacobin-style who invented the remote head lobbing by Fifth Estate drones, faith in the Monad Man the key to suppressing the towardness thinking that has any hope of our arriving together in one piece deprived of universal Tango.

ARBITRARY VIRTUE (Vespers)

He would pick anyone with whom to share his mission, anyone.
Monad Man is seed of Darwin. But since the begotten
is purely abstract, he is both unbegotten and undead, an ideal
uncreature, poster boy for the uncause recruited for.
Monad Man is Darwin's Athena, but still stuck inside his brain
like testicles that never drop from their original cavity.
Faith in his revolutionary destiny is the first doctrine propagated.
Second, all life has evolved from a common single cell.
Third, society and all things made by humans are in no way natural.
Culture, tradition in all its Cambrian variety,
is just artifice, and therefore human virtue is just a relative construct.
The three-legged stool from which hemlock is dispensed!
Only Monad Man is the natural man, a noble savage latent inside us,
an autistic feral child innocent of corrupt Society who stirs the pity
felt for misery from within, a sensibility most worthy.
(Accountable efforts to relieve misery need not apply.)
For Monad Man, social institutions have no necessary laws, no
truths, no facts that the state cannot arbitrarily adjust, and it
can meddle with traditions and laws and institutions all day.

No, duty in his name demands that the state meddle, that it strip
away the culture's artificial facade in vain hope that Monad Man
will be unearthed, Darwin's numinous missing link.
He would pick anyone with whom to share his mission, anyone.
Be neither flattered nor dismayed that he has your number.

ORGANIC THING (Compline)

Faith in his revolutionary destiny is their first doctrine.
But the Tango deals in objective science when it claims
that Logos is pulling this world toward itself, the whole world,
including that organic thing called human community.
From my tower, whose pipes have now stopped their groans,
I ponder the direction of the day's final hour.
The building maintenance man, Santiago, needed help as I came in,
help dropping a chunk of concrete into a wheelbarrow.
Our waving and heaving was a "poiein anaphoran" (poetic up-carry)
much the way the Jerusalem Temple sacrifice was offered.
I'm looking forward to a Roman emersion in my giant bathtub.
Tax day approaches, that face-to-face with my government
other than voting day, when accuracy and the thrill of hiding things
wrestle like Jacob and his angel. The angel usually wins.
"Salve Regina" is the last utterance before the Grand Silence.
Is it now all about what happens between now and then?
What happens first follows Psalm 22. Forsaken, bones counted,
a worm and no man, ends by the praising of God and the world,
a world that with Him is a seed that serves future beyond mind.

I may be visited by an ectoplasmic alien abductor tonight.
It may, at this late date, tiptoe into my bedroom,
slip between the sheets and spoon me, as if to say take me
to your leader. I will take the visitor to the Tango.

SEX AND MELANCHOLY

A Six-Poem Cycle in Favor of Social Security Reform

or

Reflections of a Mandarin Baby Boomer

Sex and melancholy are tall in youth's
pursuits and capacity. Wasted on the
young, though. Now, when we know
too much about sex and have more
reason for melancholy, when we'd
be ruling the one (if only we could get some)
and become the perfect slave of the other
if only youth's vigor had not jumped ship,
we are the great over-qualified masses.

We are the unwashed cutting edge gone dull.
We are the blooper on your disaster screen . . .
We, the boomers, be tsunami here.

My voyages are of no consequence.
Whether I, the real first admiral of
the Ocean Sea, am never so known to you
or whether I get headlines: "His charts
opened the world to its true dimensions,"
I am nothing. I am safer in anonymity.
May the evidence otherwise stay buried.
What matters is saying the proper prayers
for the dead and accurately predicting

the next holocaust. This is the work
of we, the boomer generation, not a lick of
difference from the most benighted savages.

By the time I've applied all the creams
to prevent my skin from erupting like
Spartacus, and have strapped on all the
tourniquets that keep the blood at bay
and brace the failing ligaments and bones,
I've placed myself under the Principle
of *Stare Decisis* precisely because
I was raised among Confucian mandarins.
In my youth, though, I shipped out with

The emperor's eunuchs, sailed around the
Cape of Good Hope and across the
Atlantic to found a New World Press.

Utopia was my soya beans and rice,
my pomelos and lime, my gin and tonic
all at once. If I ever doubted Utopia,
I had only to belly up and slap down cash
and/or bring to mind the Forbidden City.
The emperor's armada alone was a floating
paradise. Eight hundred gigantic nine-masted
treasure ships in massive convoy,
each with sixteen internal watertight

compartments, any two of which
could be flooded without sinking it.
Trained otters herded shoals into our nets.

Concubines were housed in balconied cabins
adjacent to sixty different state rooms below
where ambassadors of Persia and India,
Malaysia and Africa, each entouraged by
ten *chefs de protocol* and fifty-two eunuchs,
would hold court in style on the high seas.
Before and after such passengers, the empty
cabins converted to laboratories and classrooms
for the mathematicians, astronomers, engineers,

architects, metallurgists and botanists,
historians and poets, cartographers, all sent
by the Dragon Throne for global research.

From wine press to printing press,
Utopia burned strong for us all, until
the Doomsday Book arrived. Its electro-
techno syntax was foreign to our natural
semantic retrieval methods. And now we
can either throw ourselves into syntax mind
or cultivate old semantic mind in secret.
Heaven has since struck the Forbidden City.
When we returned, no one knew our name.

We are the last holocaust. Foretold
on gum wrappers and scrawled graffiti,
the next boom you hear will be my whimper.

ABOUT THE AUTHOR

American poet and performer Tad Cornell (T. H. Cornell) was essentially an underground poet after his first book, *Glance Over at These Creatures,* was published in 1977. Some of his writing was distributed conventionally, but more was personally bound and hand-gifted, presented in poetry slams and avant garde stage productions (in Hong Kong, Houston, and Philadelphia), and on guitar and vocals as part of a poetry fusion rock band, Edgar Allen and the Poettes, and other ensembles.

Cornell's childhood until age twelve was in Germany where his father worked for the US State Department (as a CIA agent, Cornell later learned). A child opera star at the Frankfurt Playhouse, he was featured in the Boy Scouts magazine *Trailblazer*. After high school in suburban Philadelphia, he earned a BA in English from Temple University, a master's degree in special education from Antioch College, and a master's degree in English literature from Villanova University. The special needs of his only child, born with spina bifida, led him to a thirty-year career in social work. At intervals along the way, he was drawn to consider the priesthood, served as a Trappist novice in the Abbey of the Genesee, and studied theology in Rome at the Angelicum.

ALSO BY TAD CORNELL

The Needle's Eye: Sonnets to Cristo (Juggling Teacups Press, 2016)

In Whom Is My Delight (Juggling Teacups Press, 2015)

The Unspeakable Mating (Latitudes Press, 1989)

Honey From the Rock & Hong Kong Elegies (Latitudes Press, 1988)

Glance Over at These Creatures (RHD, 1977)

CHAPBOOKS

The Graphics of the Mouth (2006)

Gloria Über Alles with Stan Heleva (script and score, 1999)

It Seems Important (1988)

The Promise of Silence (1978)

Rosie Knuckles Knows (1978)

Cough Poems for the Tickle (1978)

Looking the Moon in the Face (1977)

Hollywood Diamond Exchange (1977)

Marco Polo (1977)

Made in the USA
San Bernardino, CA
21 December 2015